This
Coloring Book Belongs To

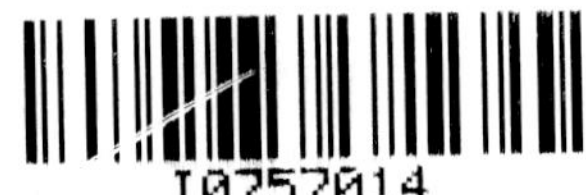

Color Test Pages

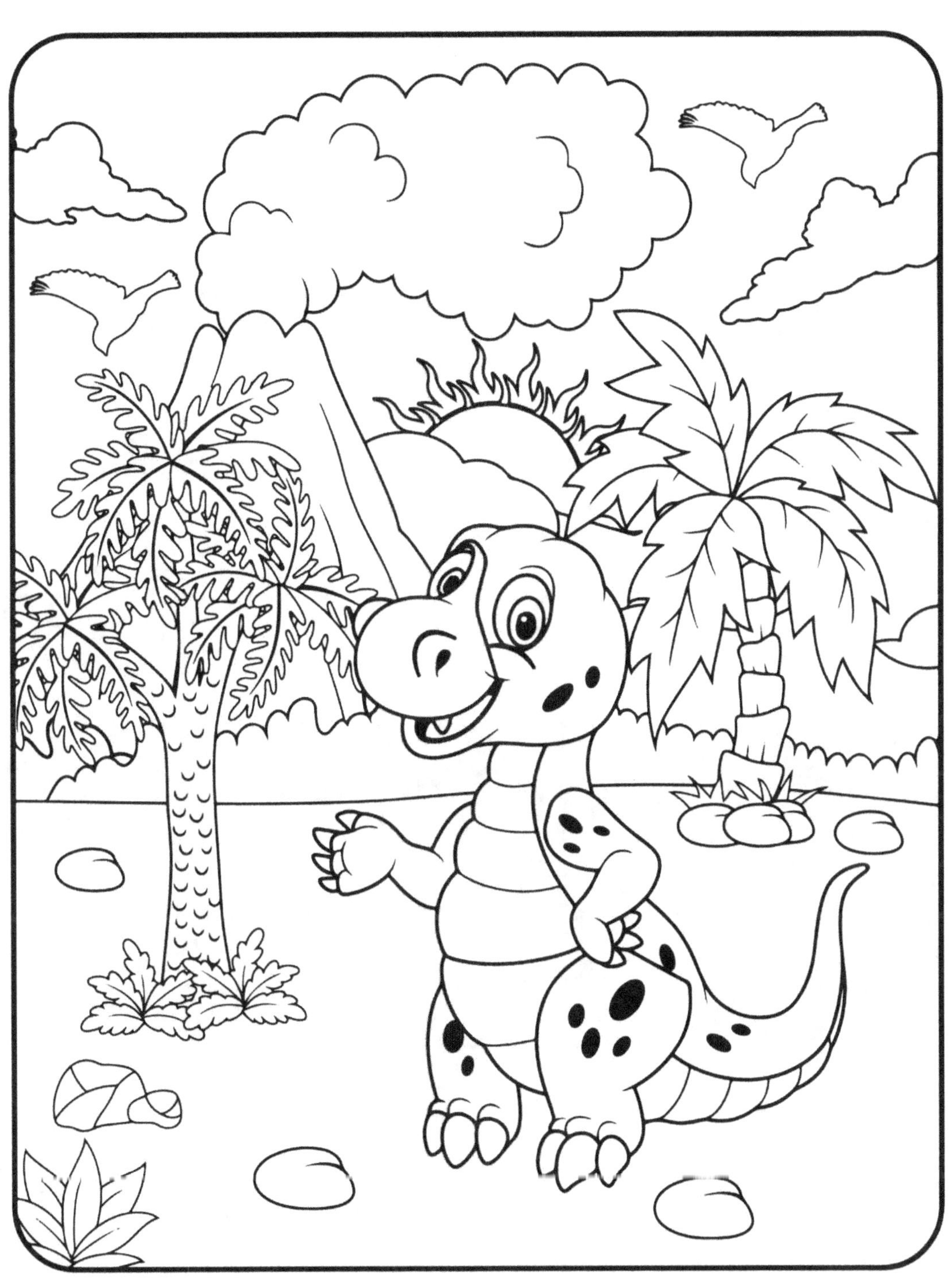

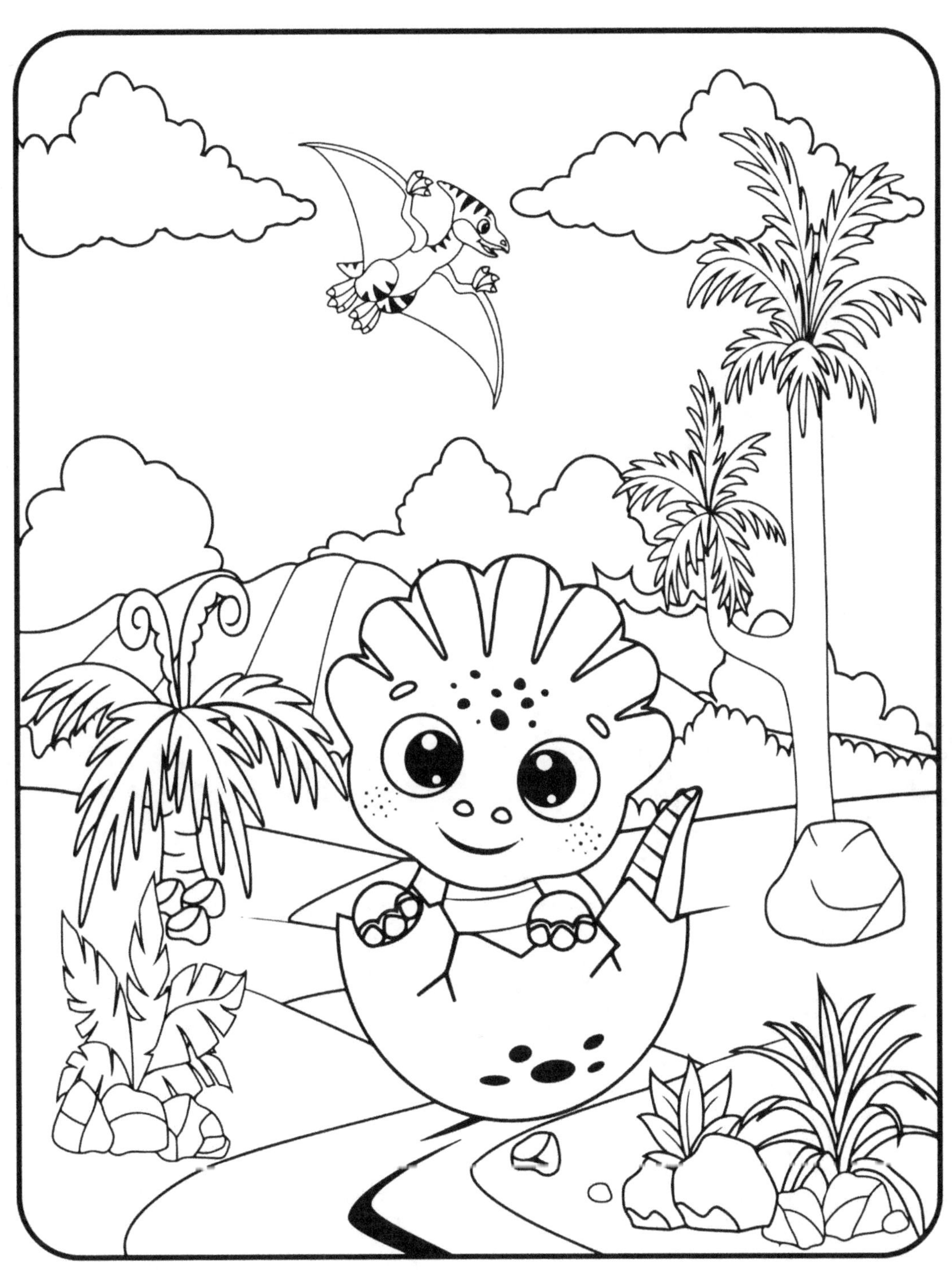

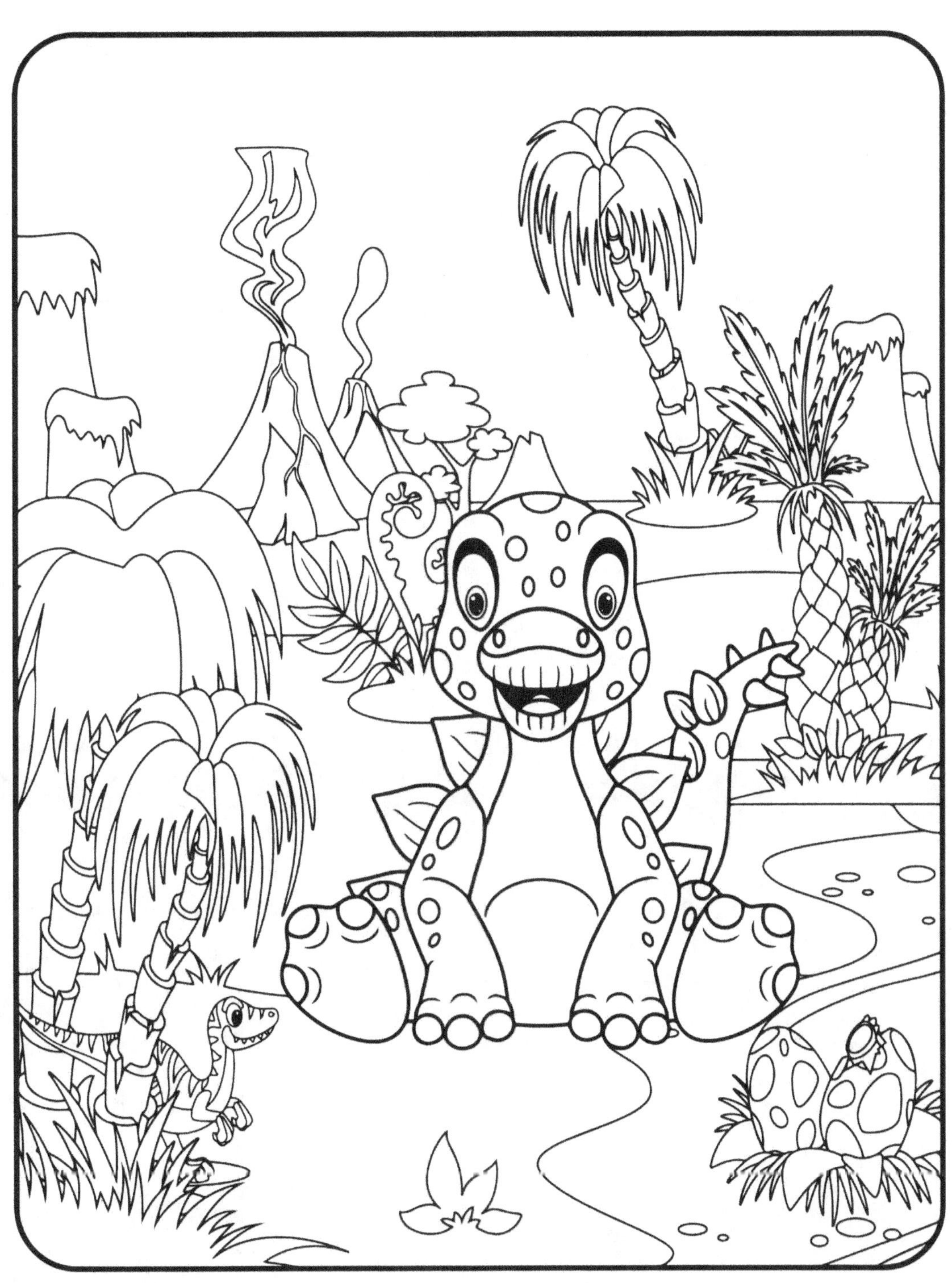

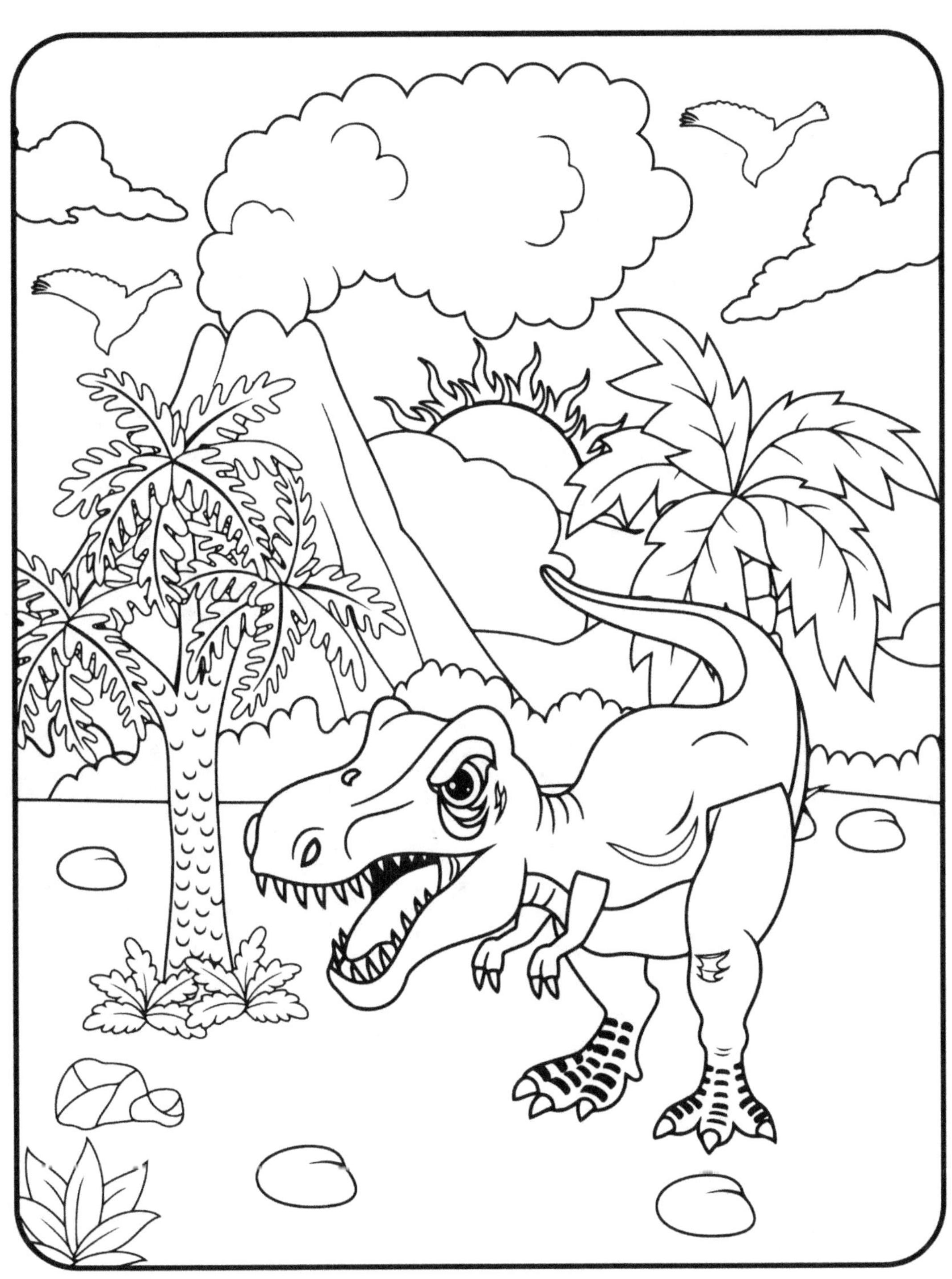

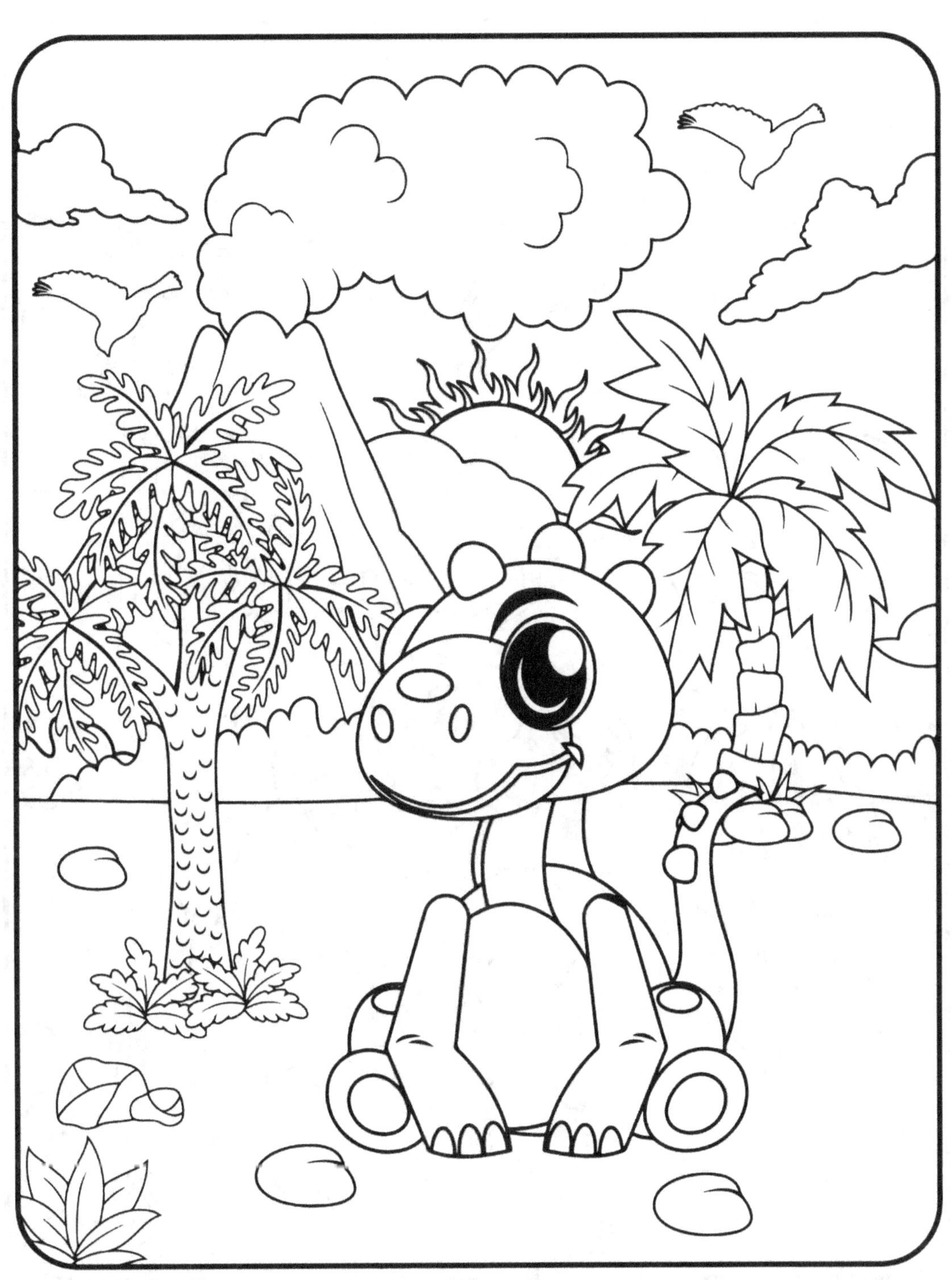

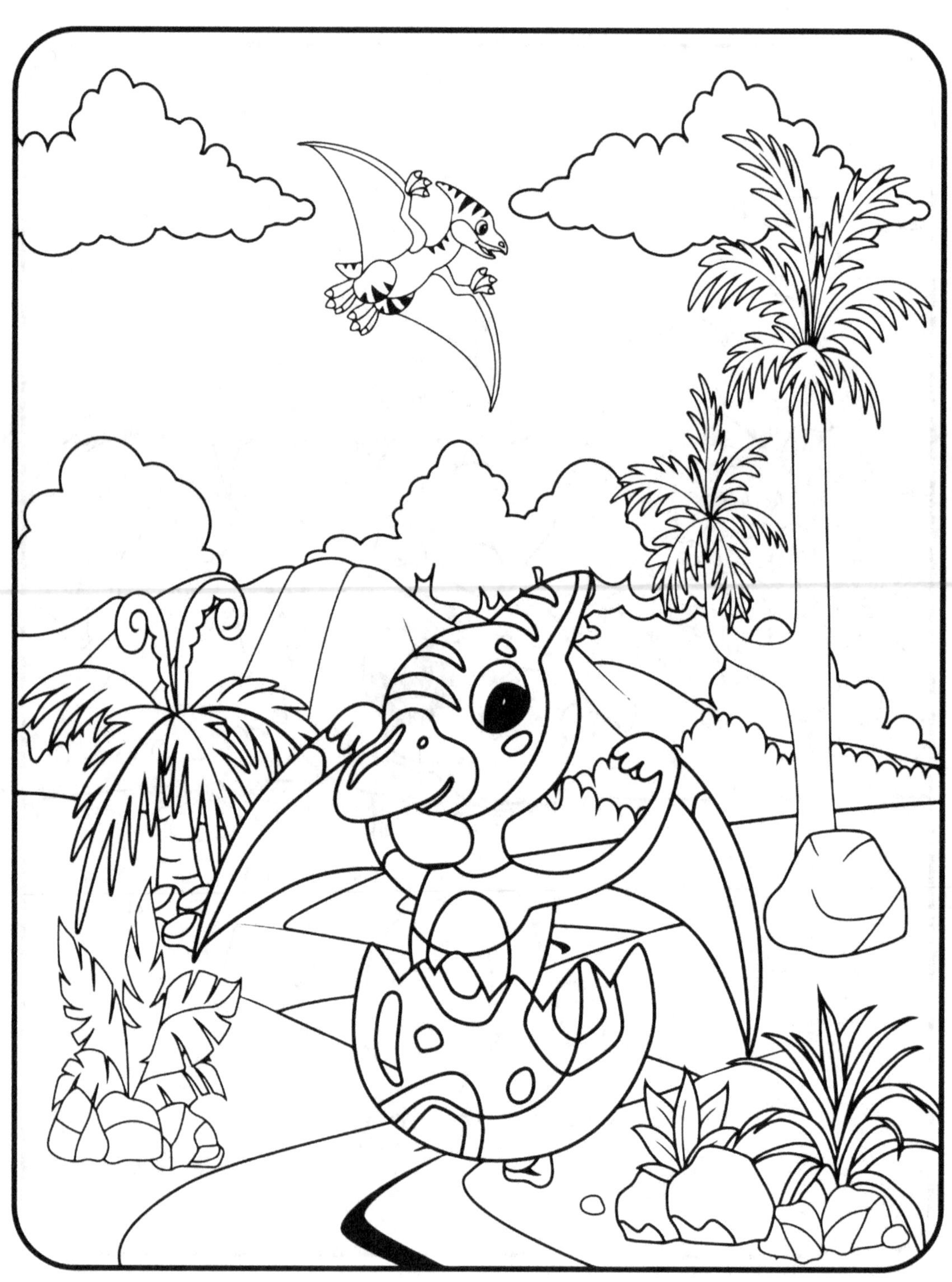

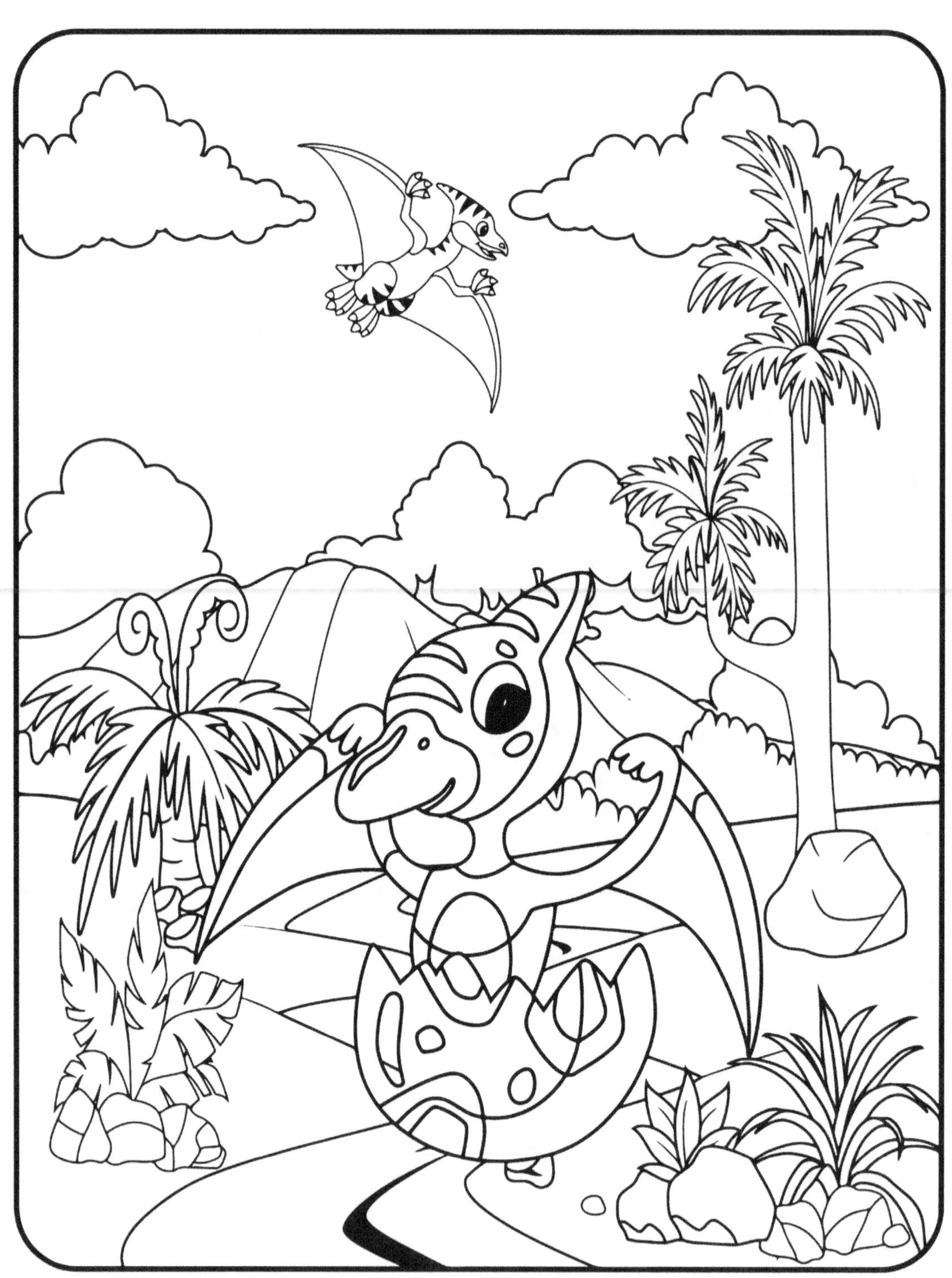

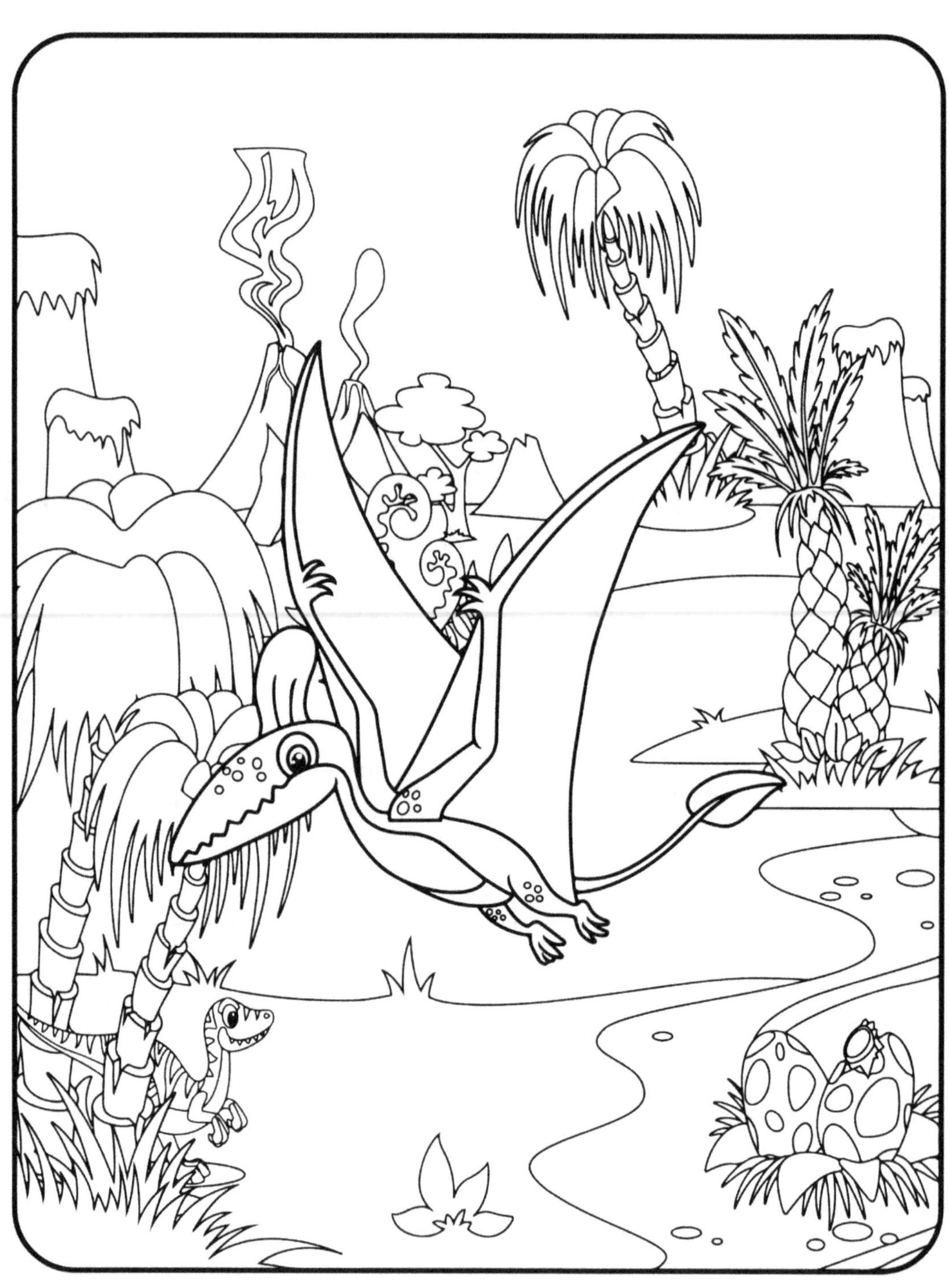

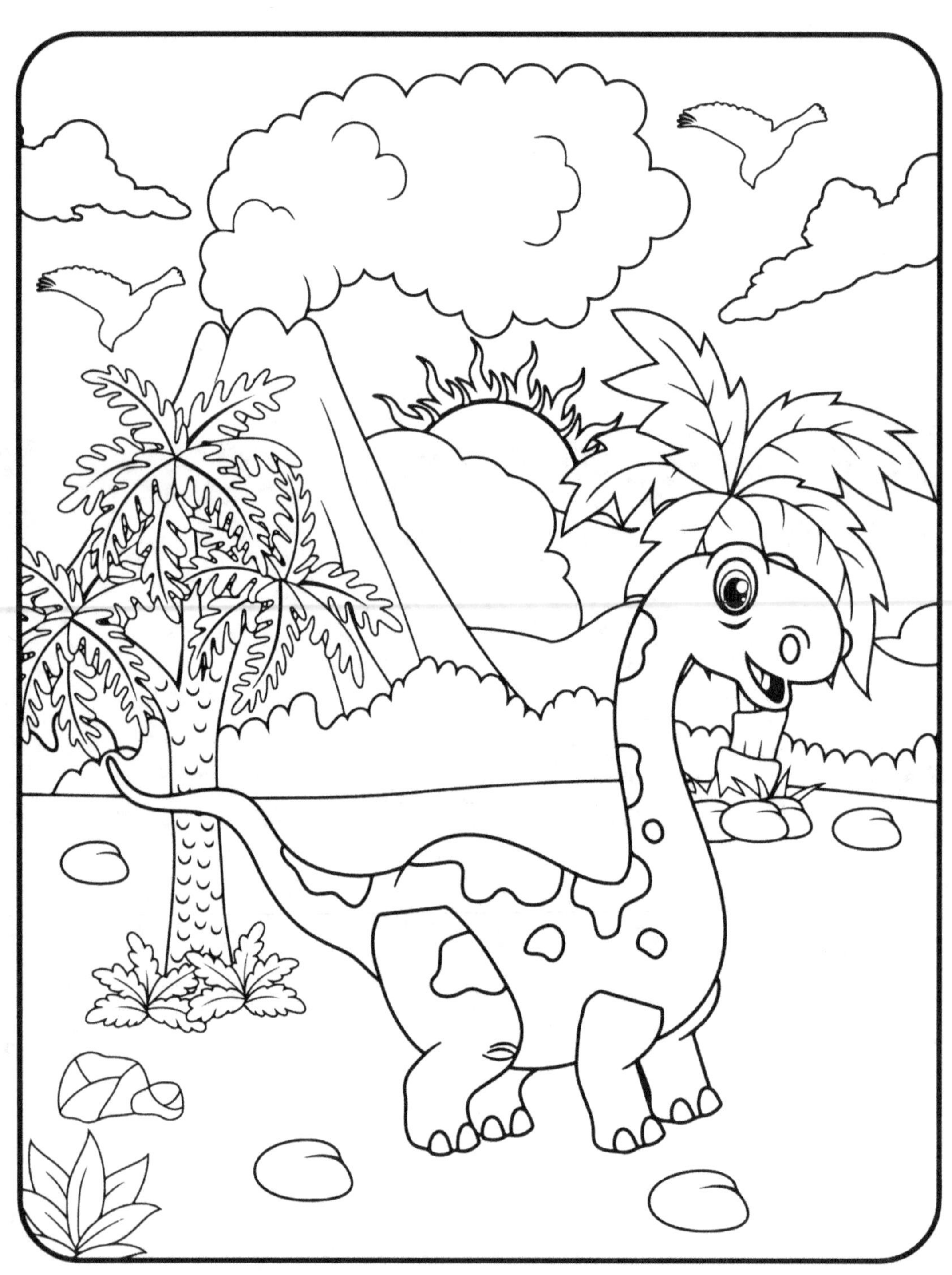

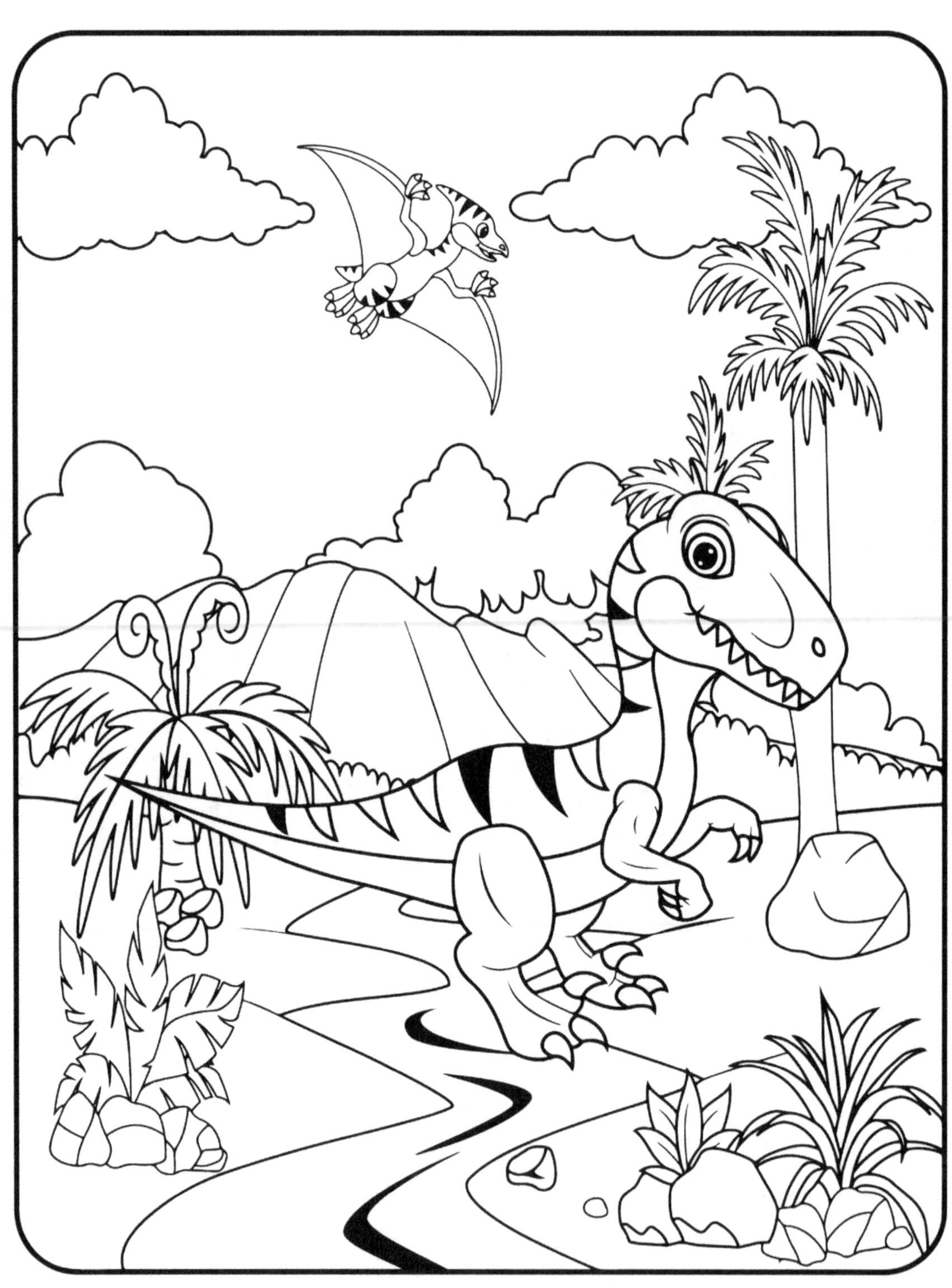

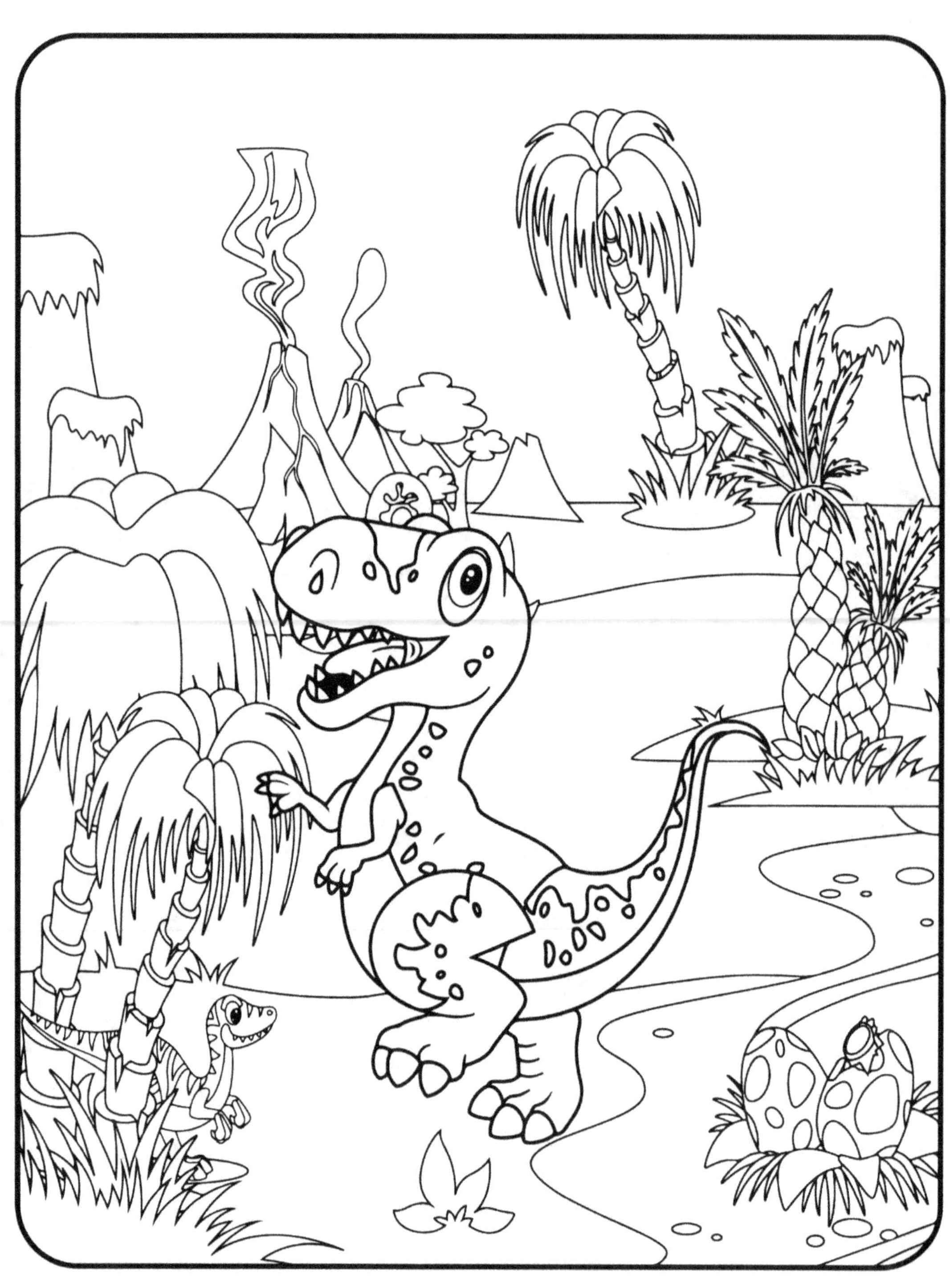

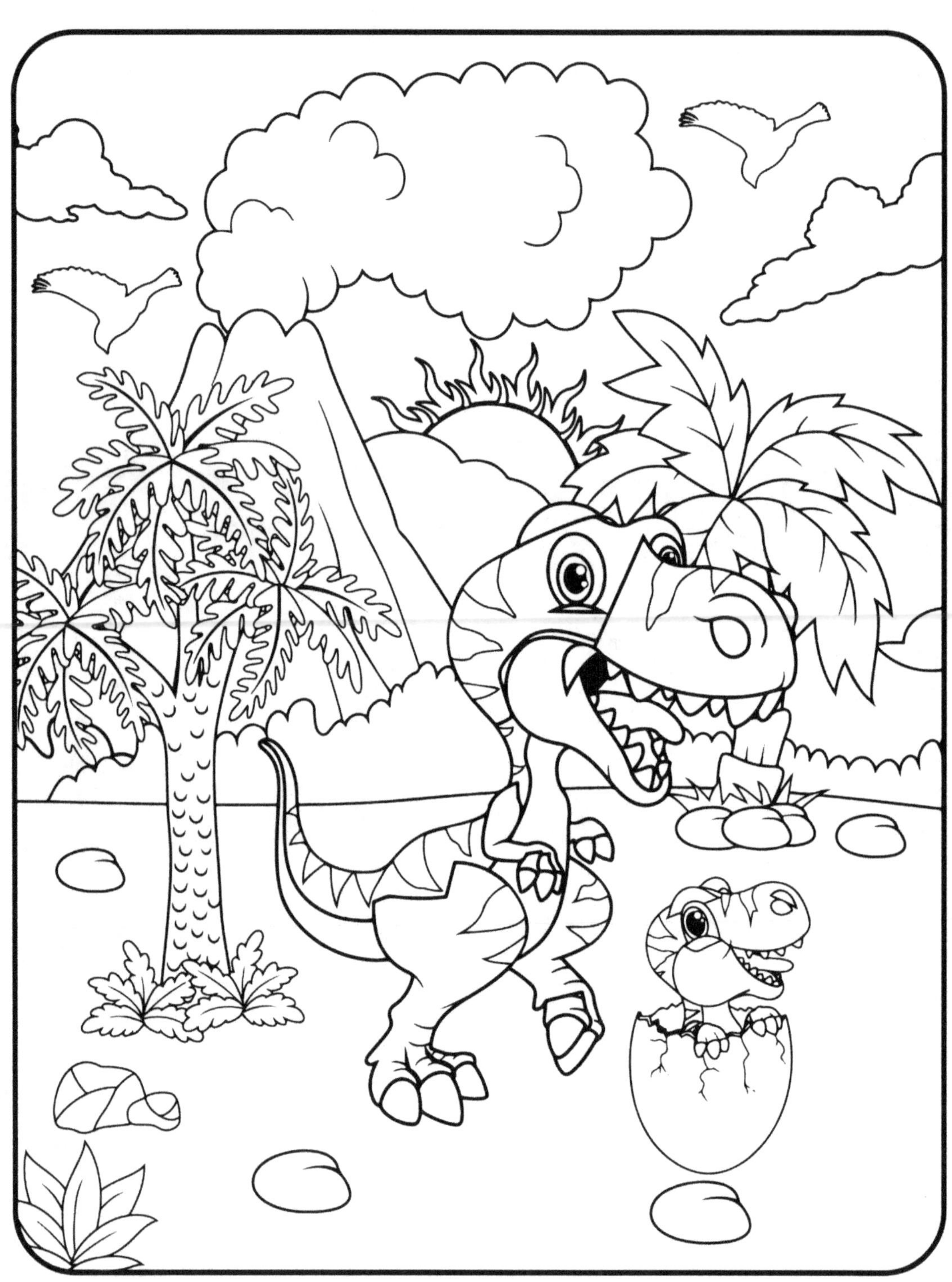

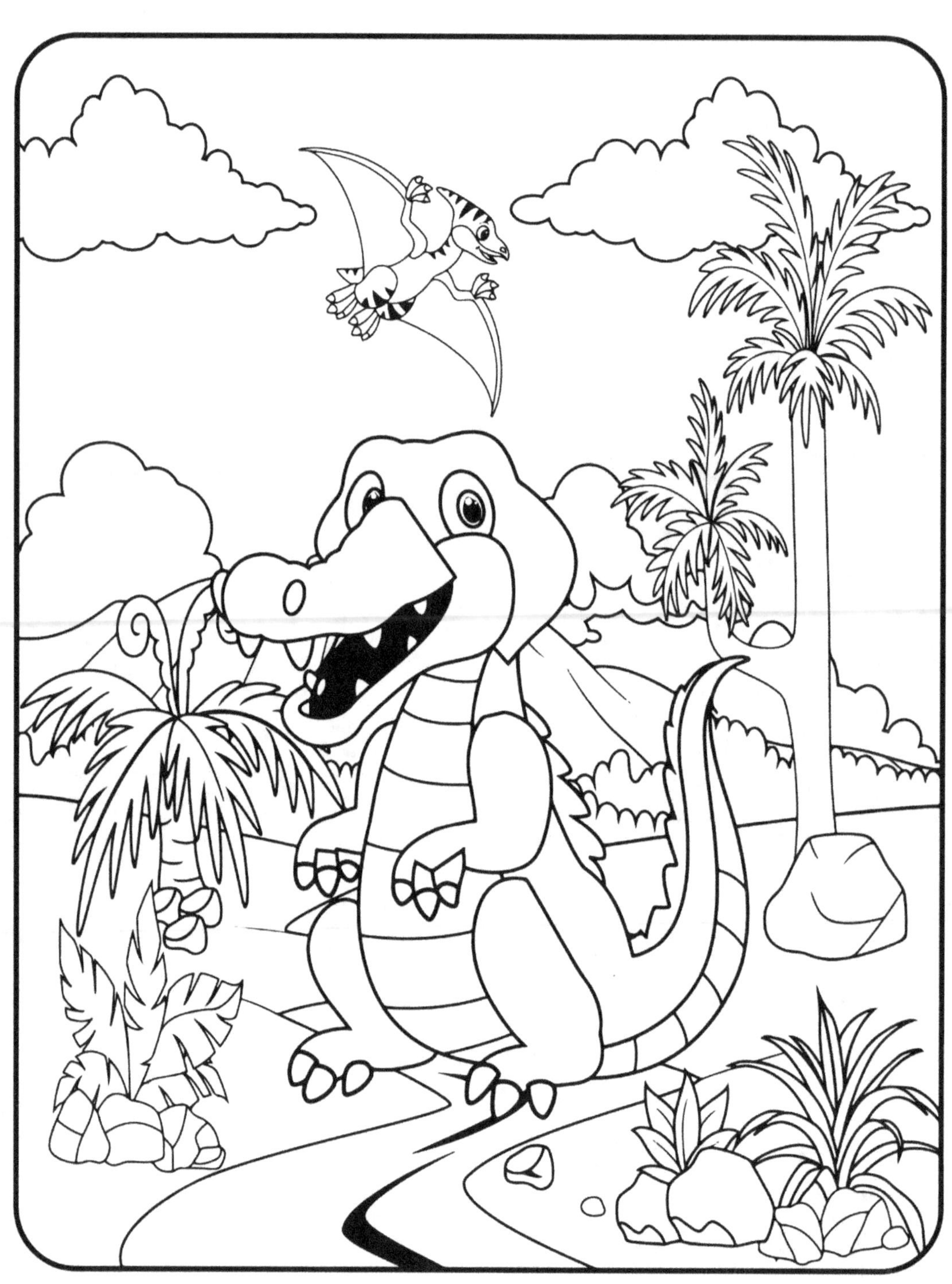

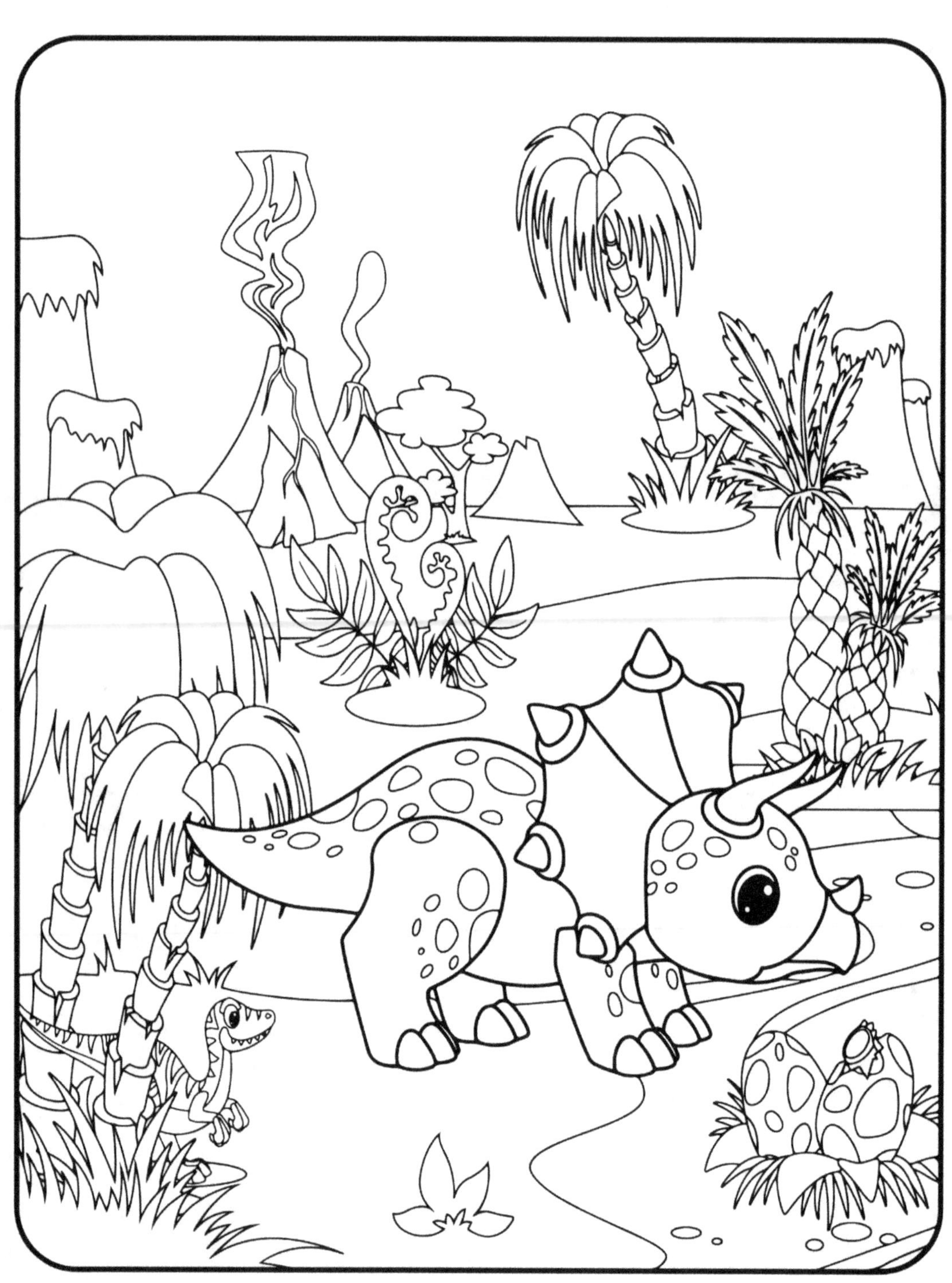

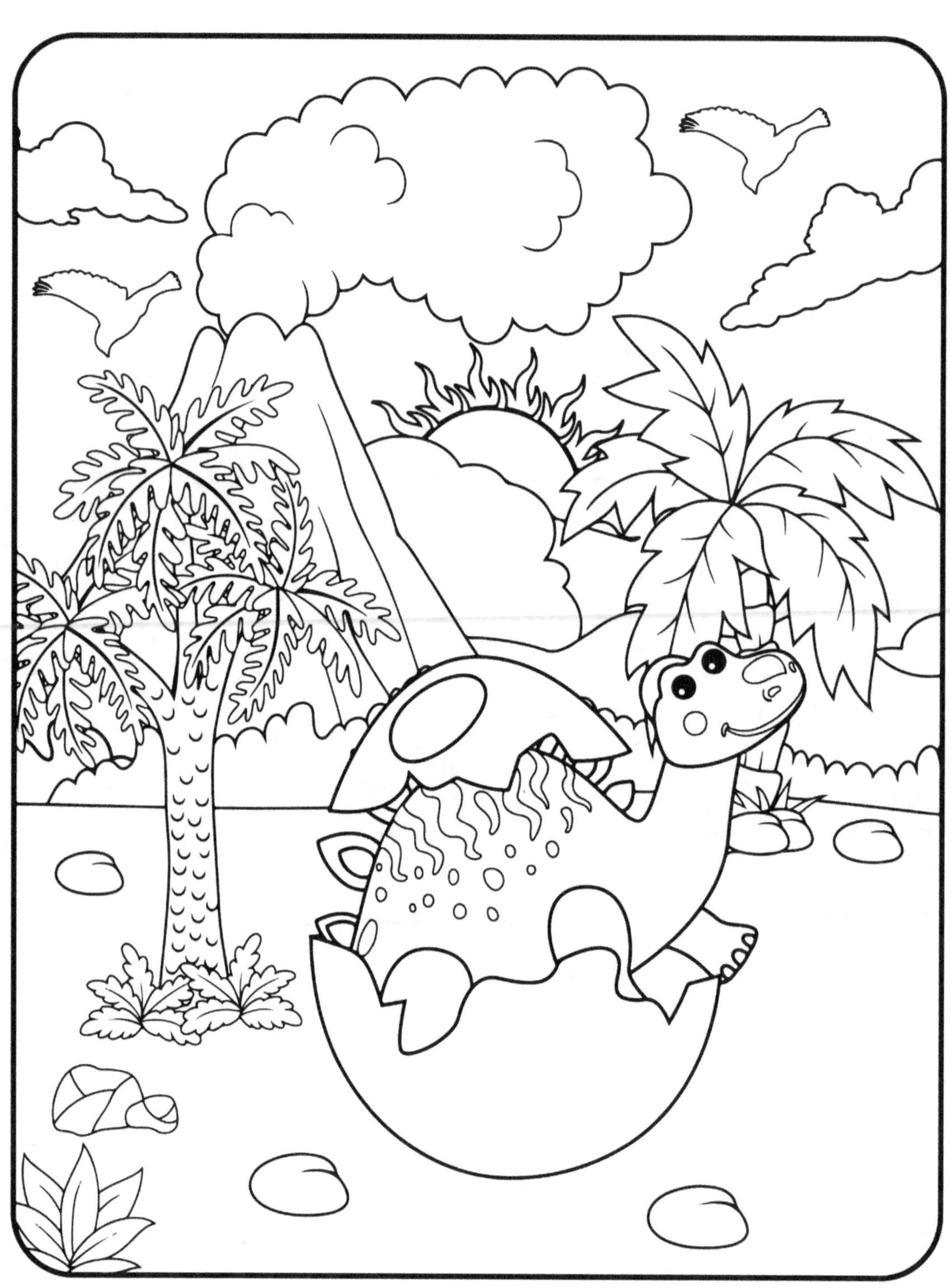

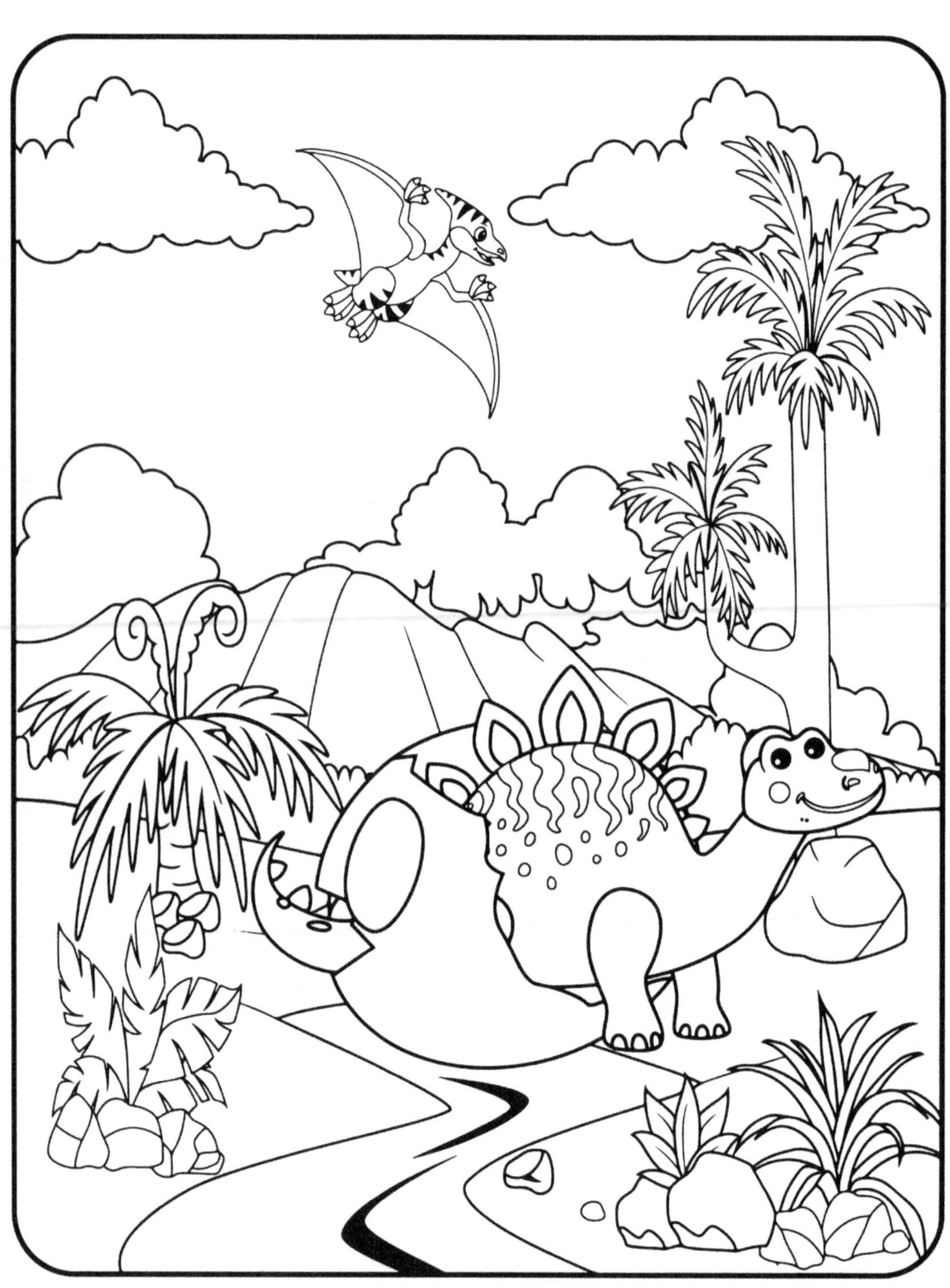

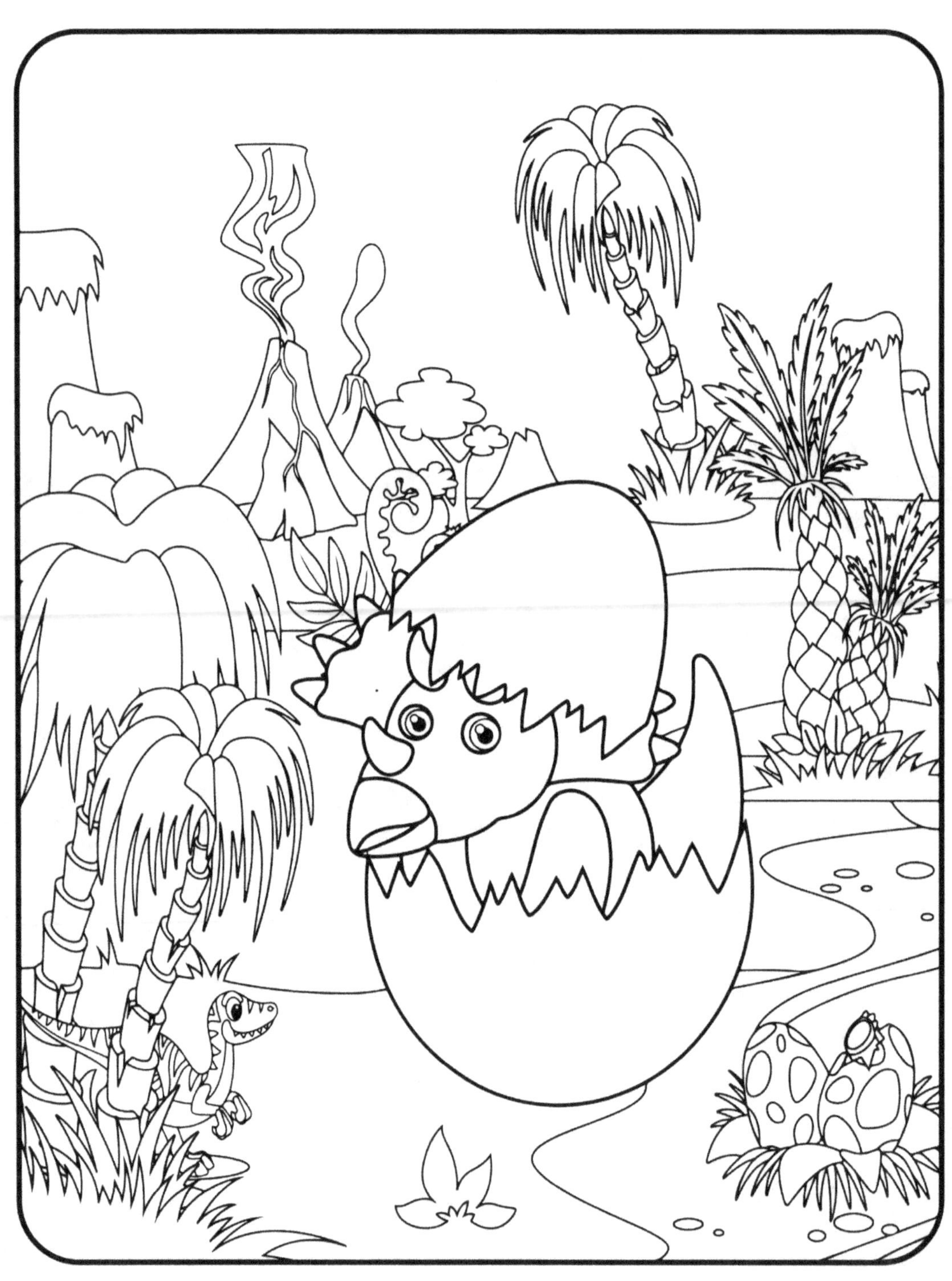

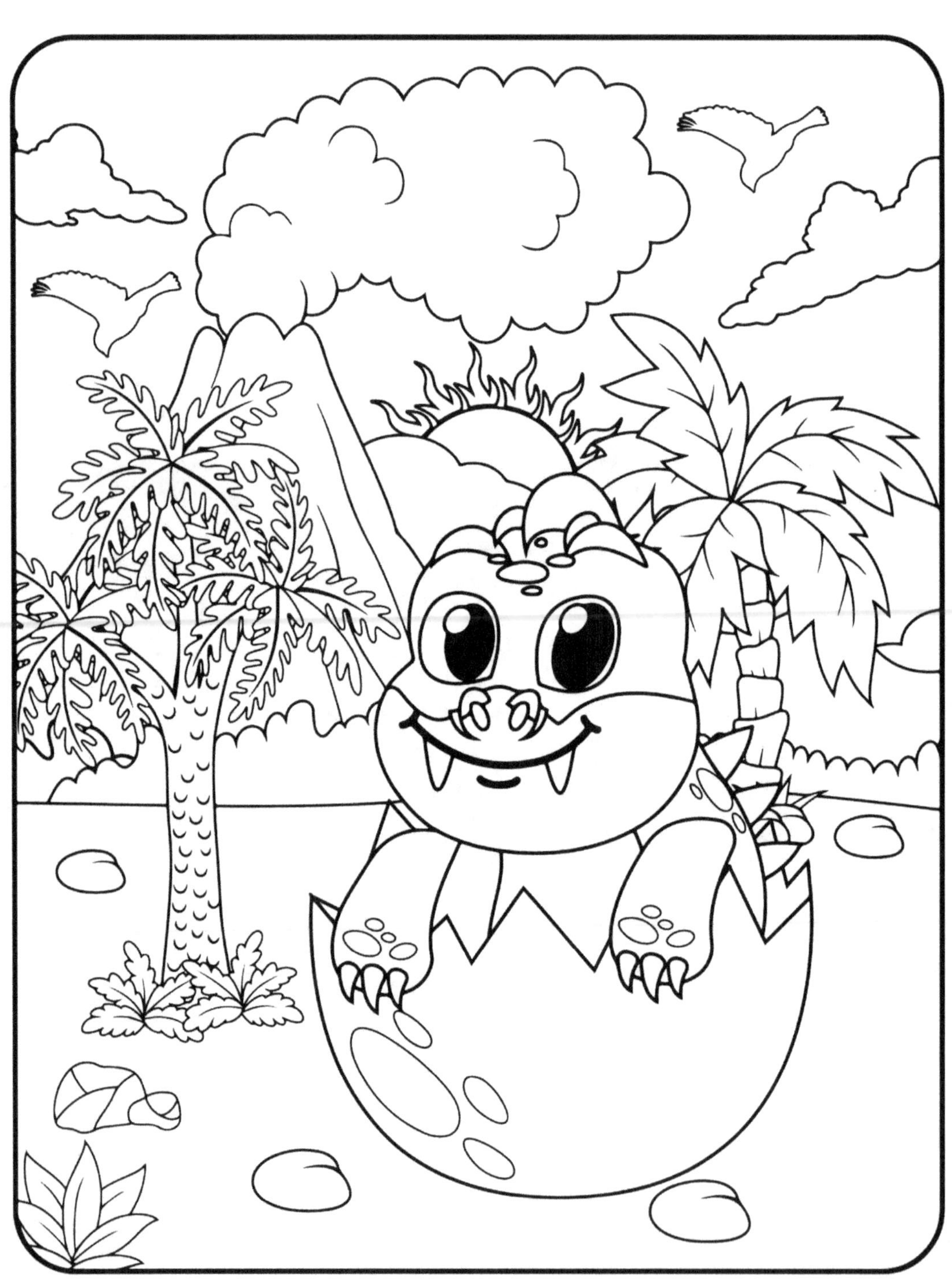

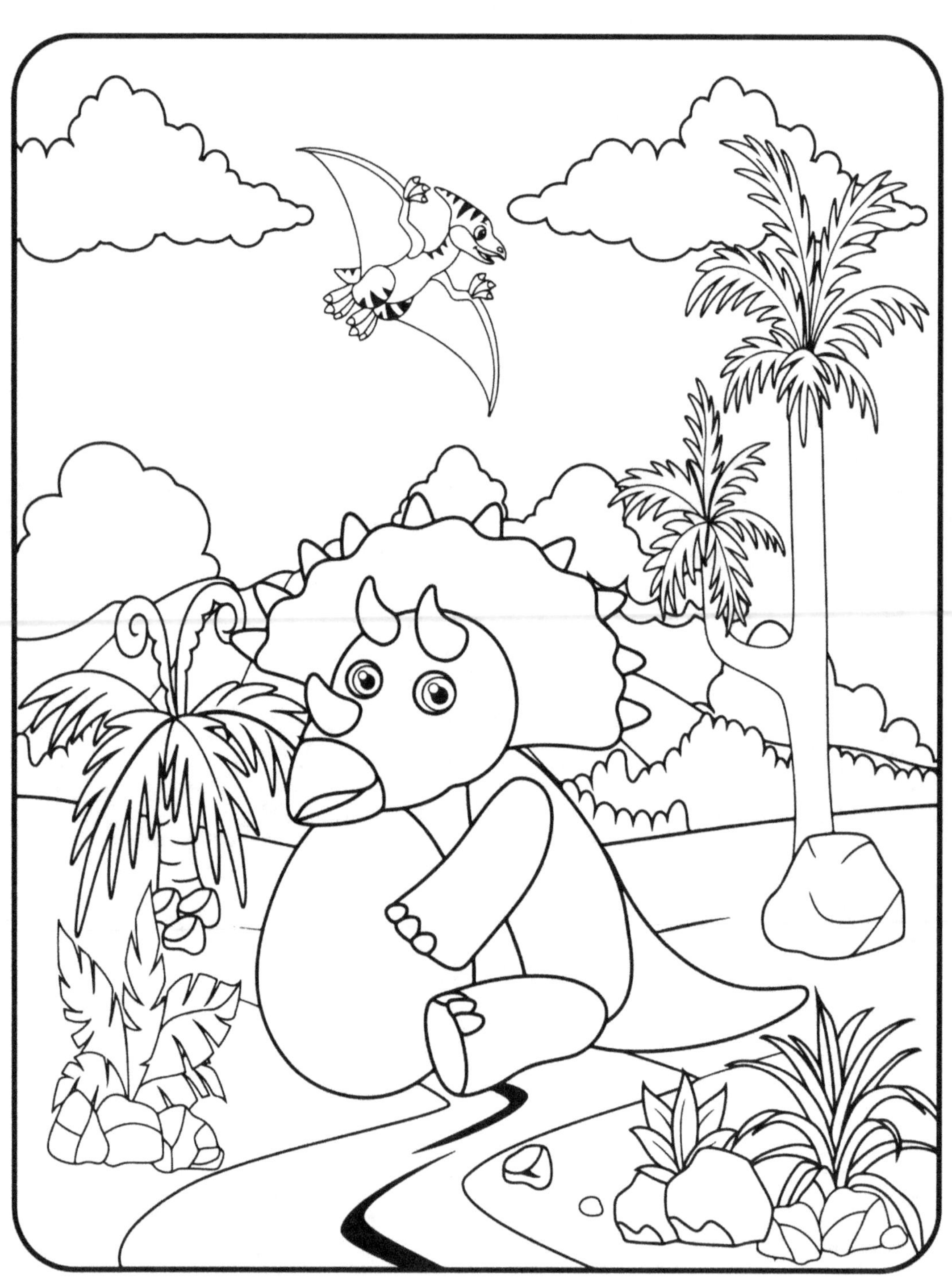

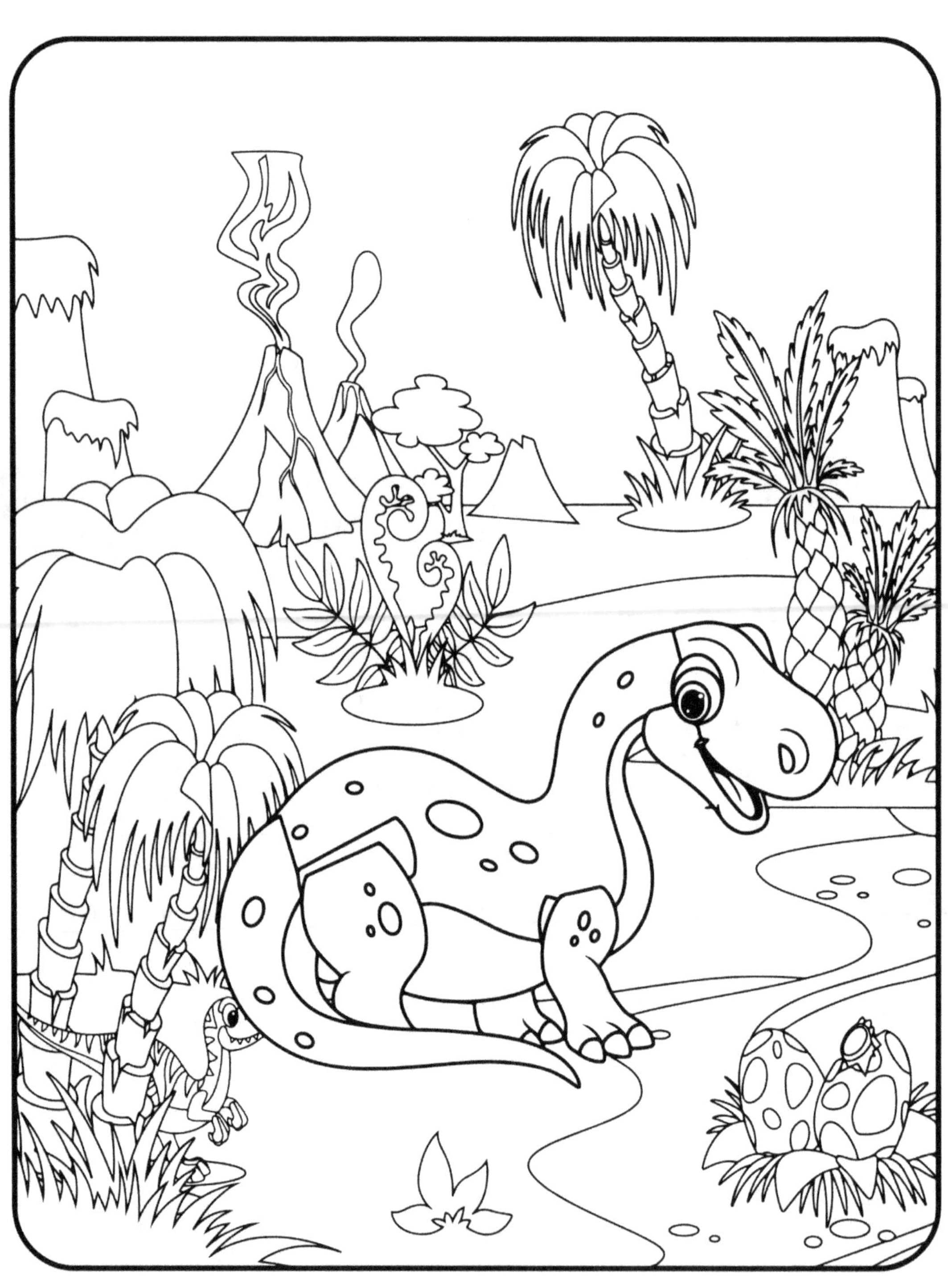

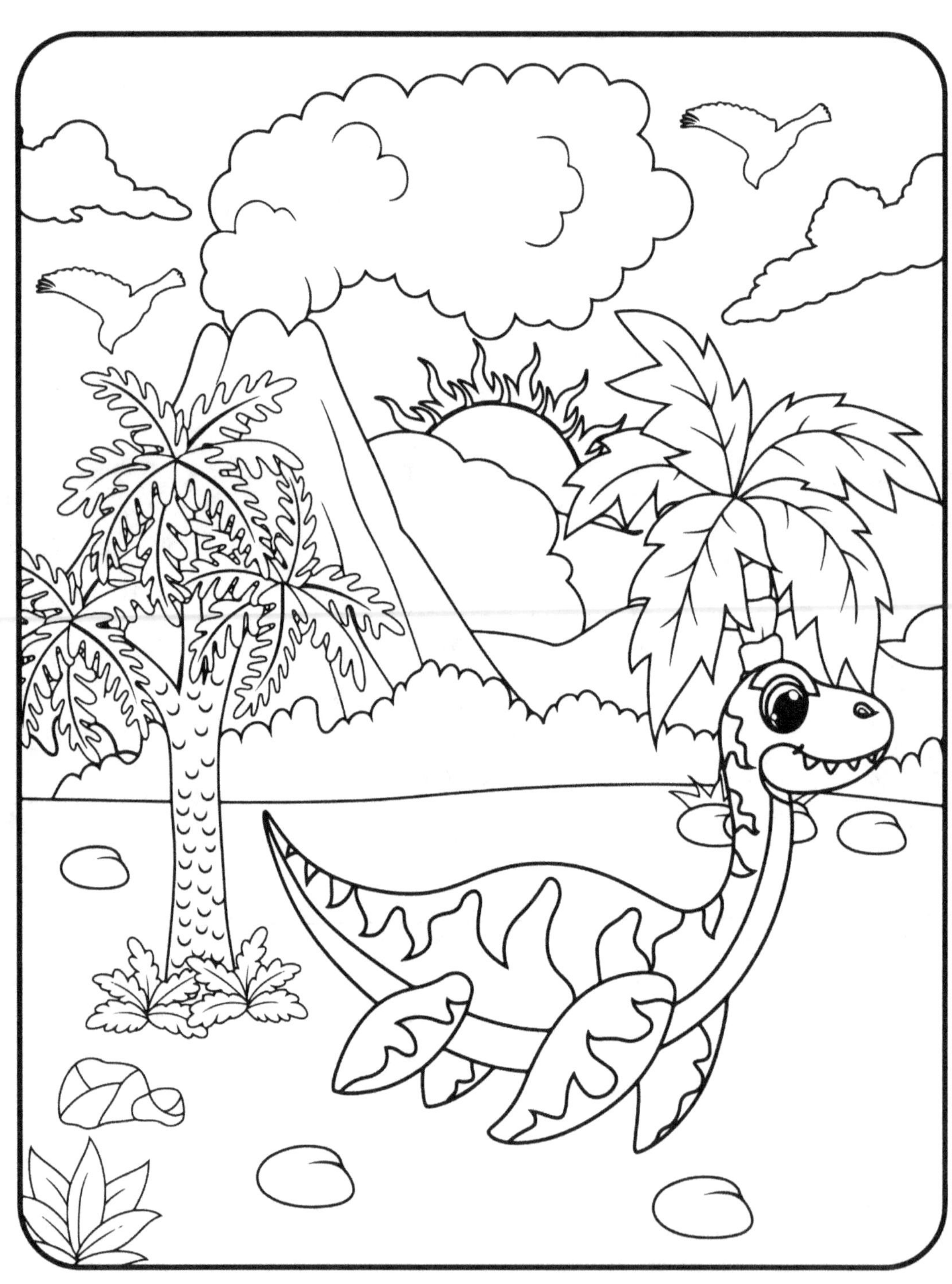

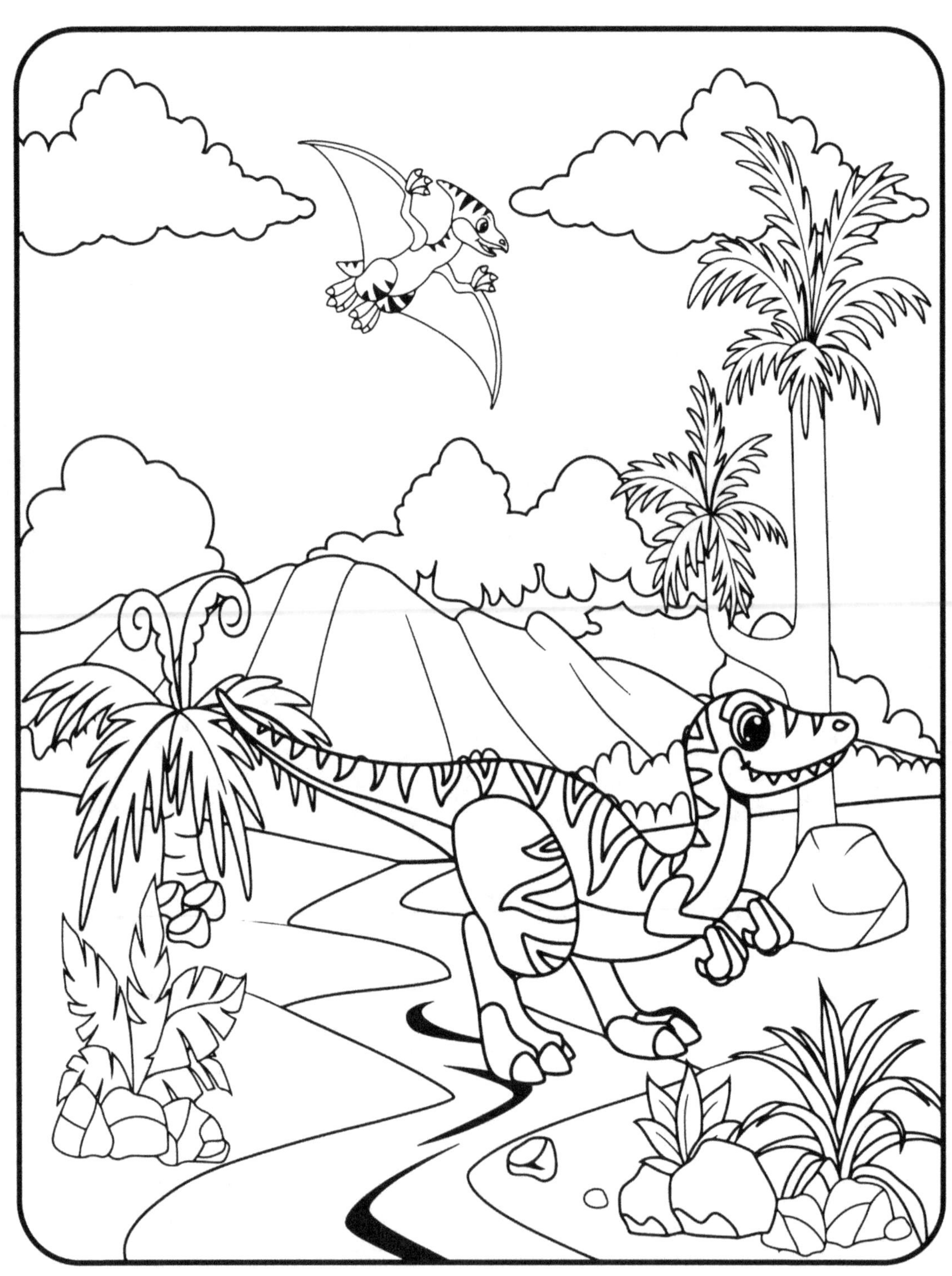

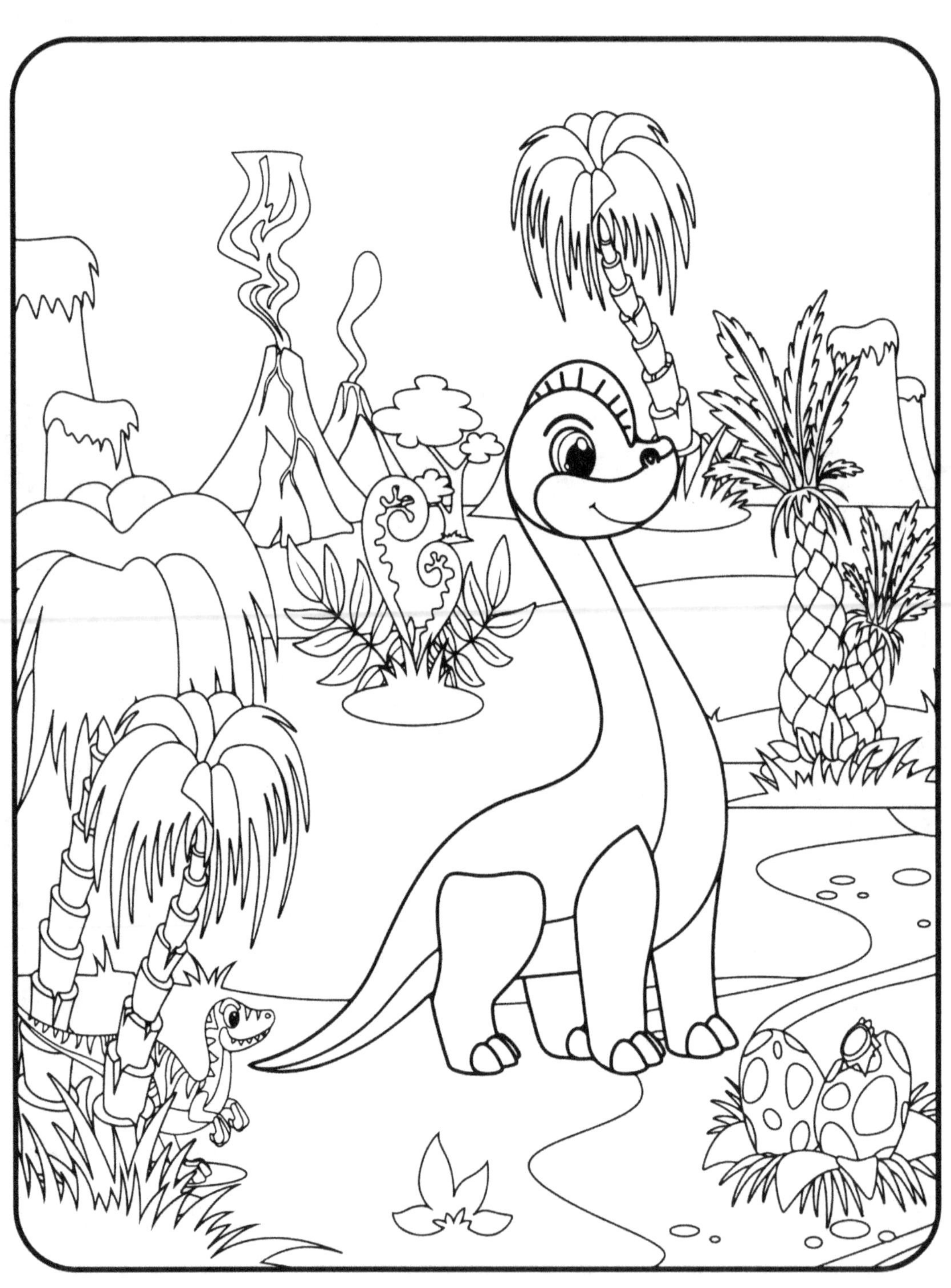

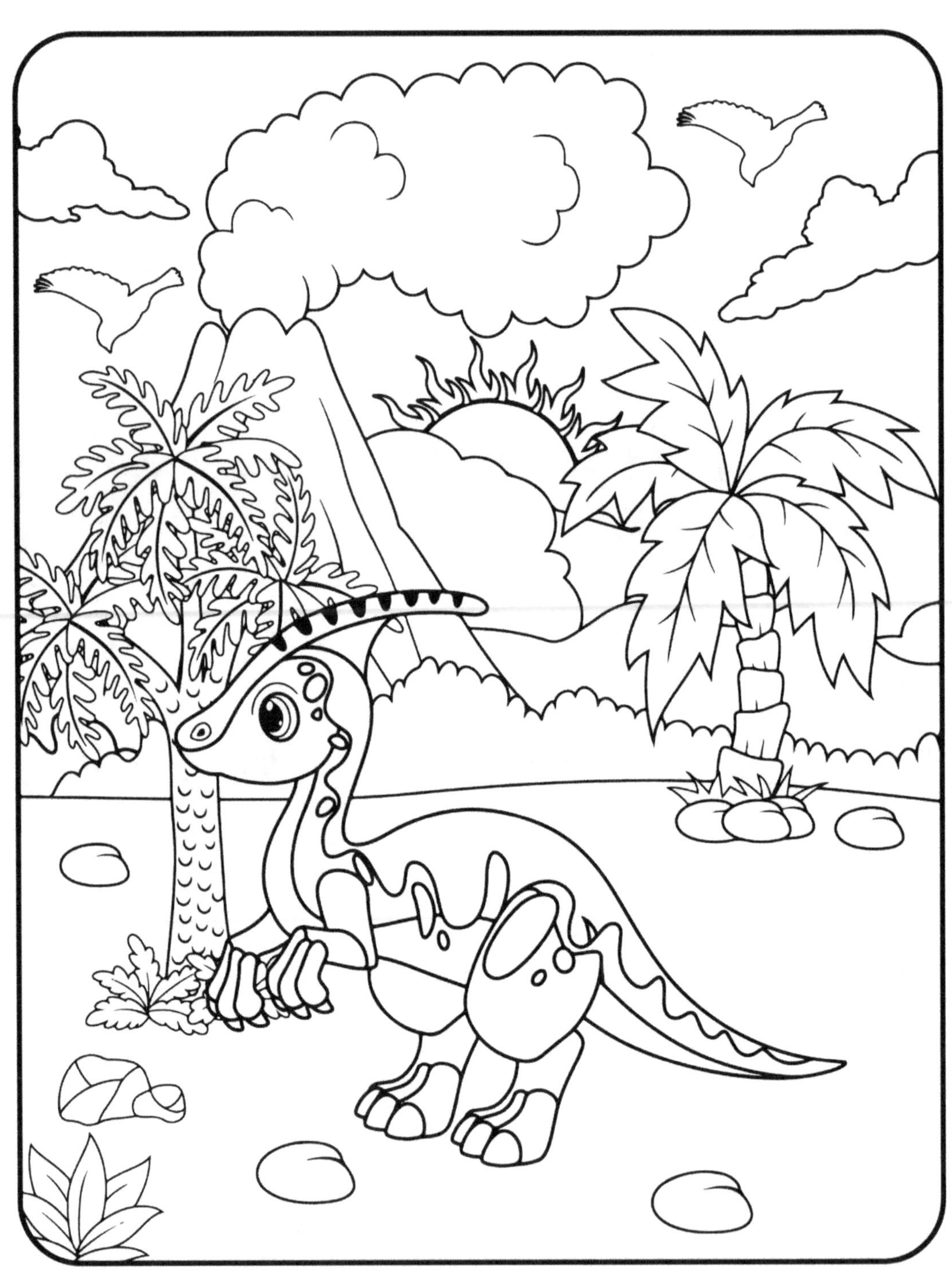

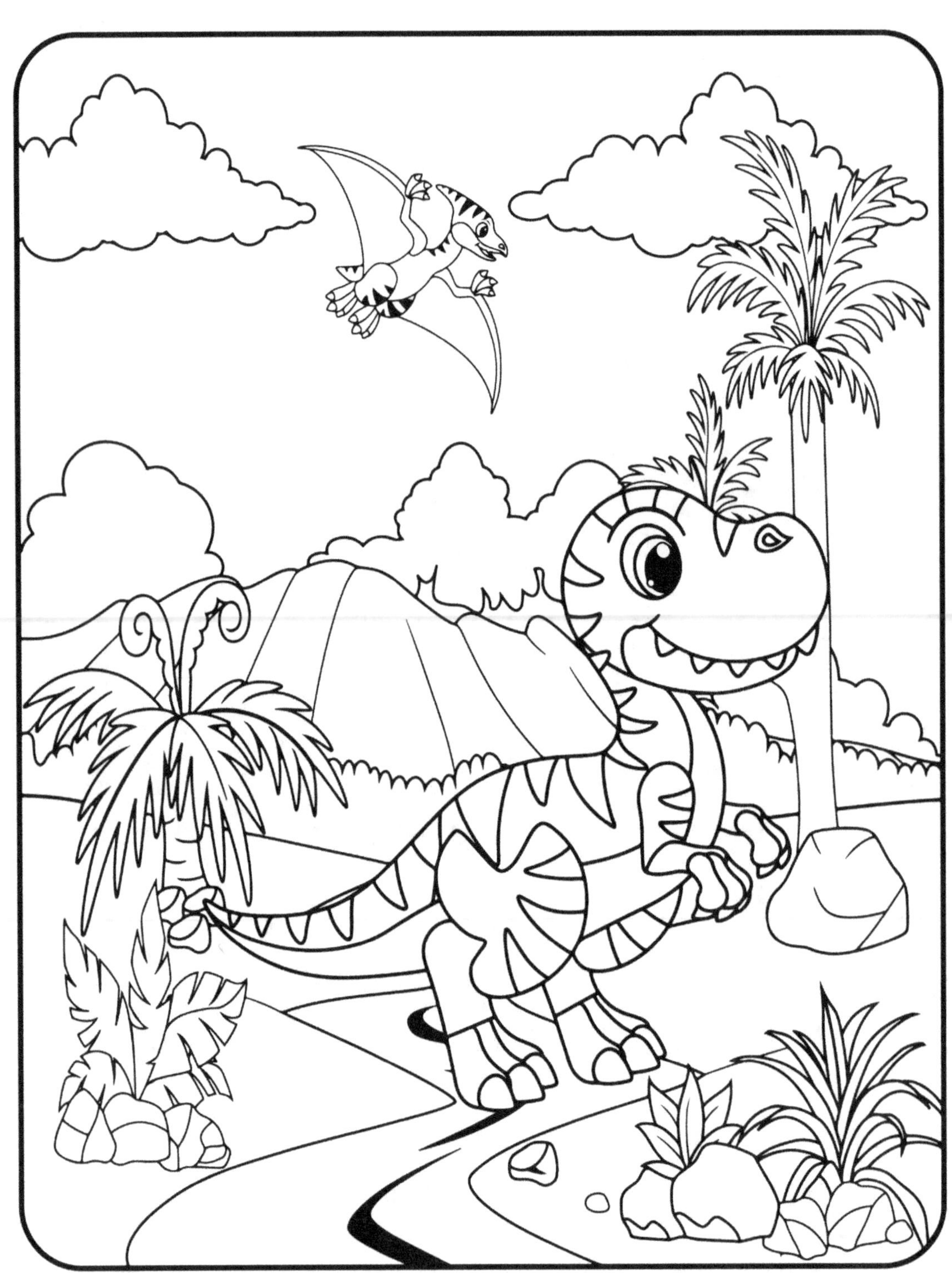

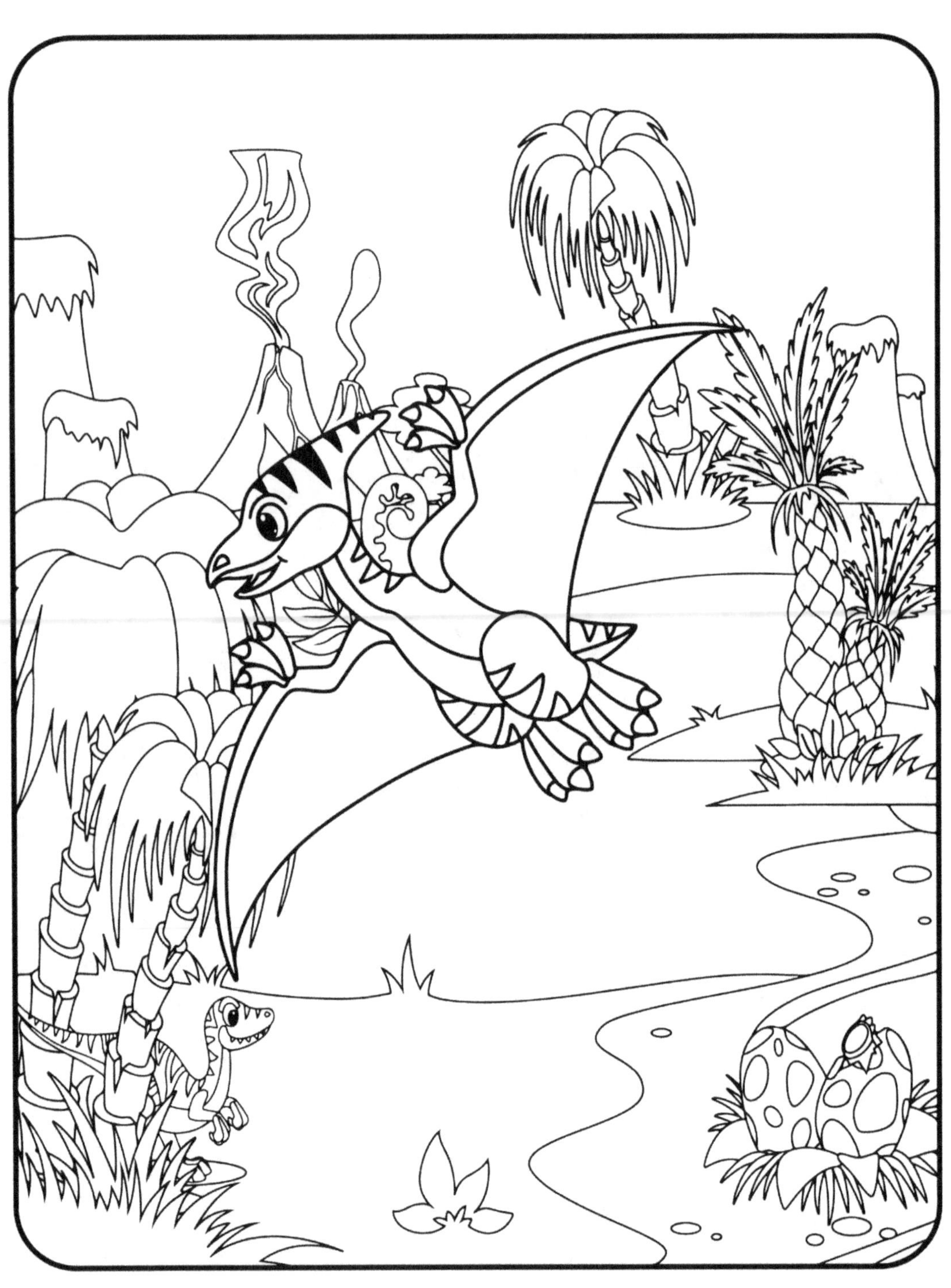

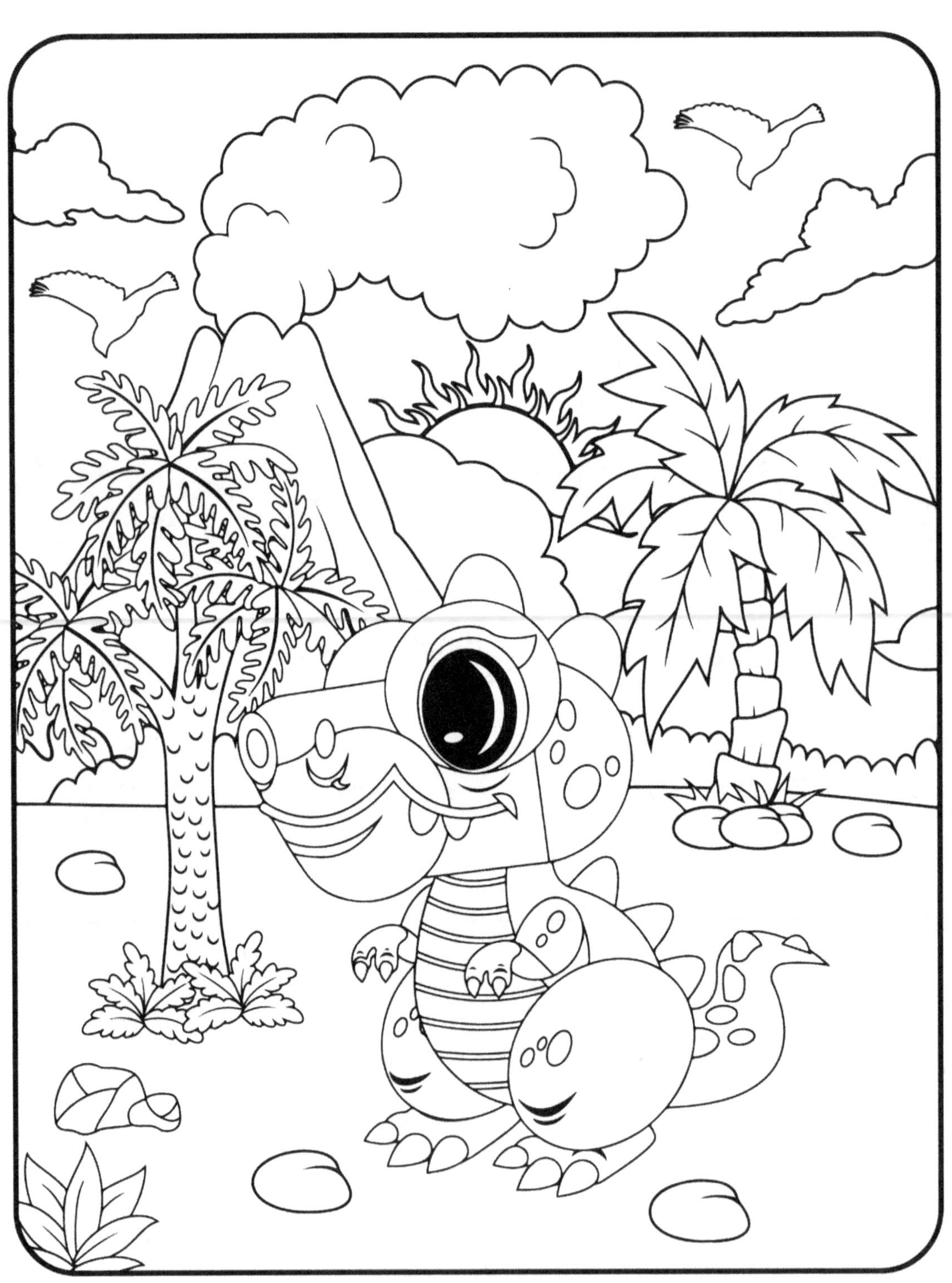

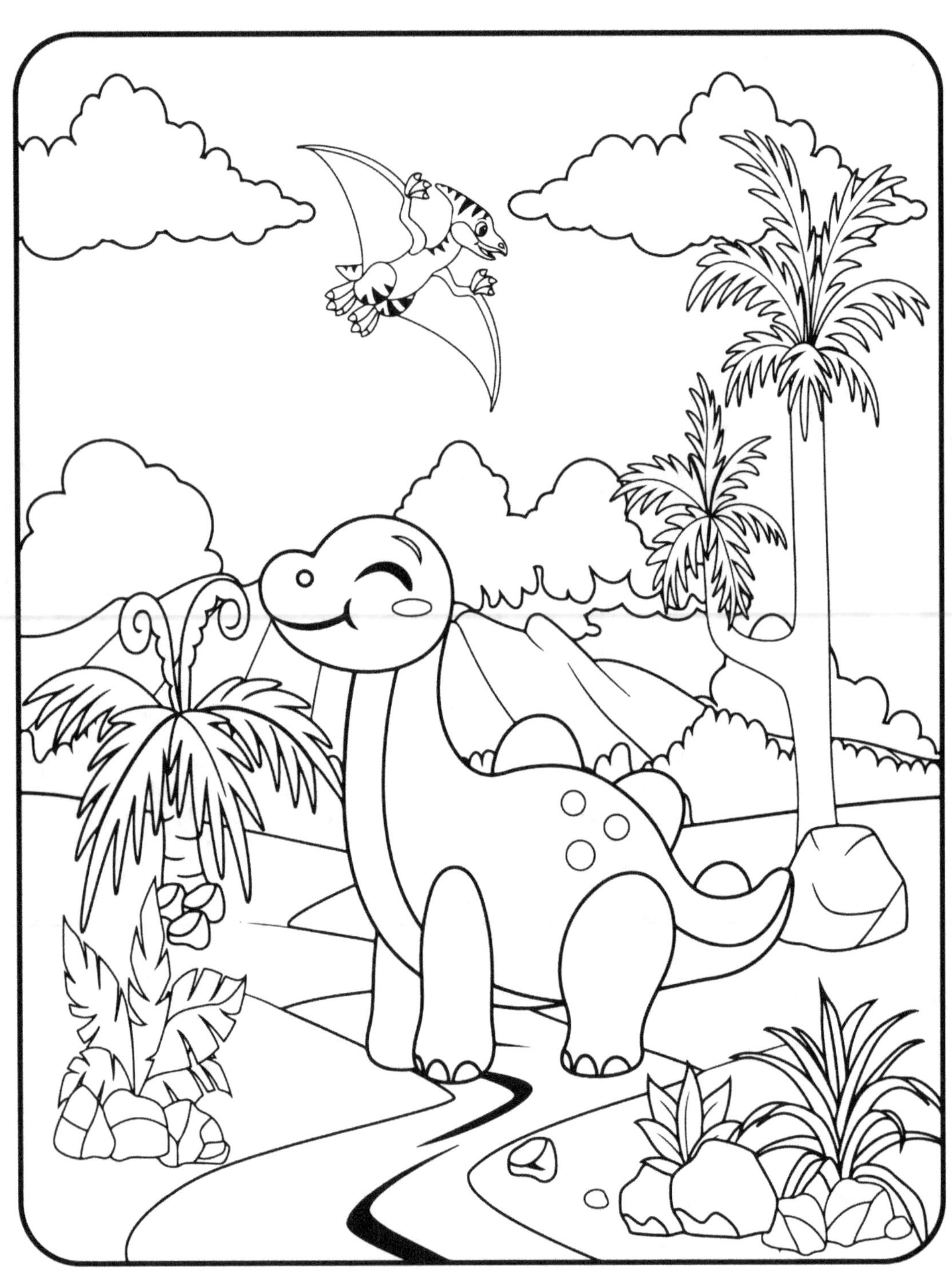

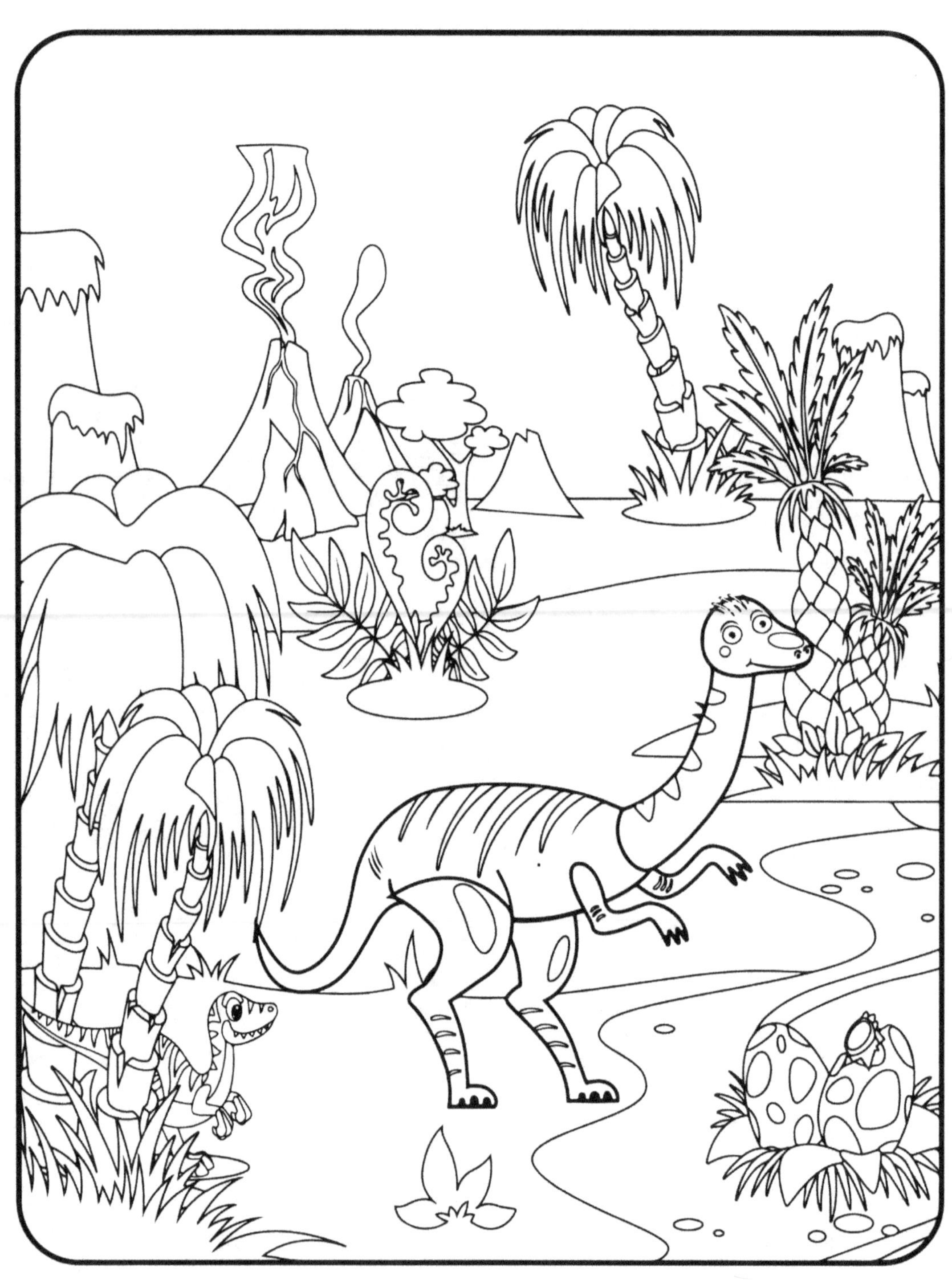

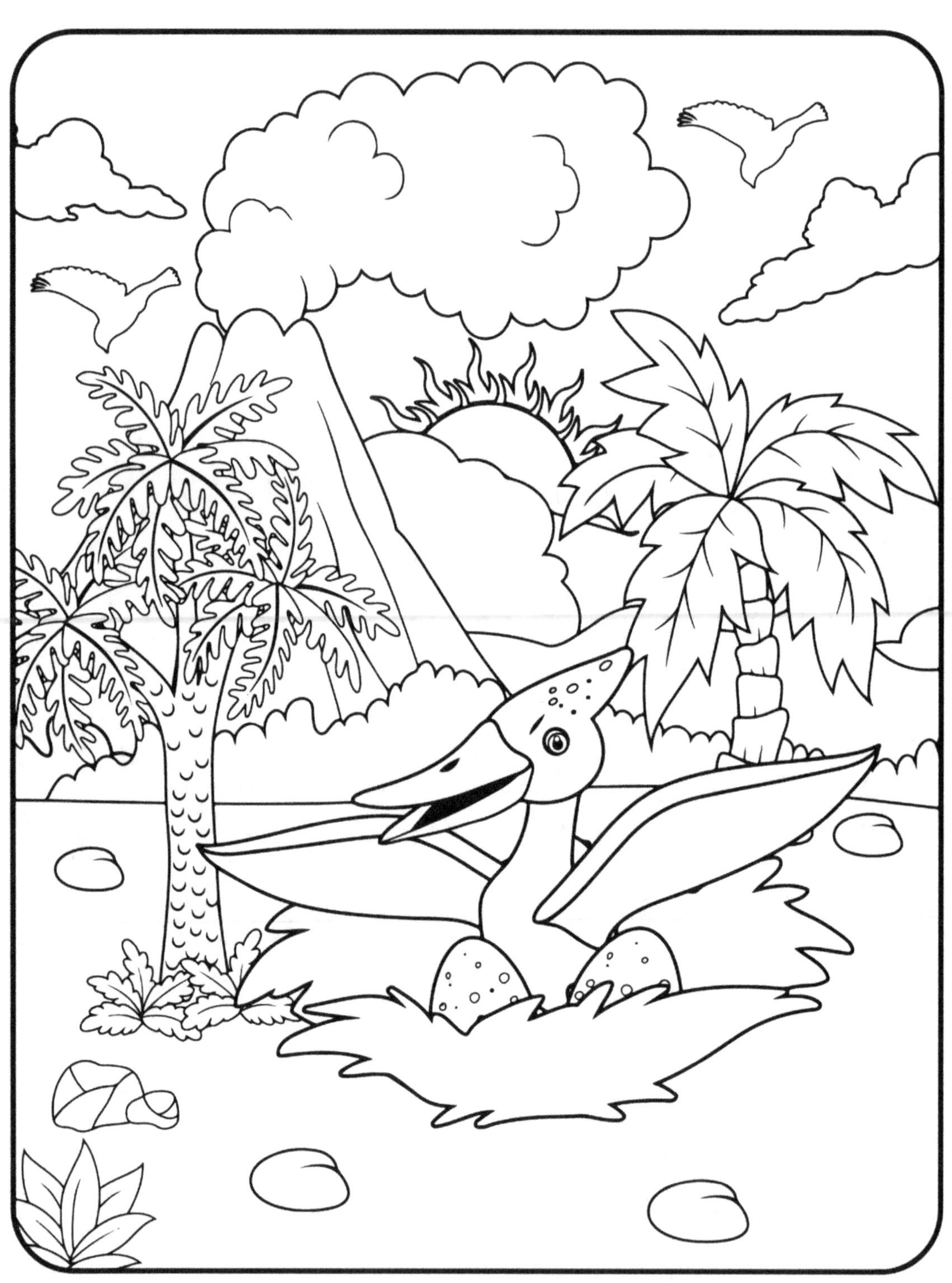

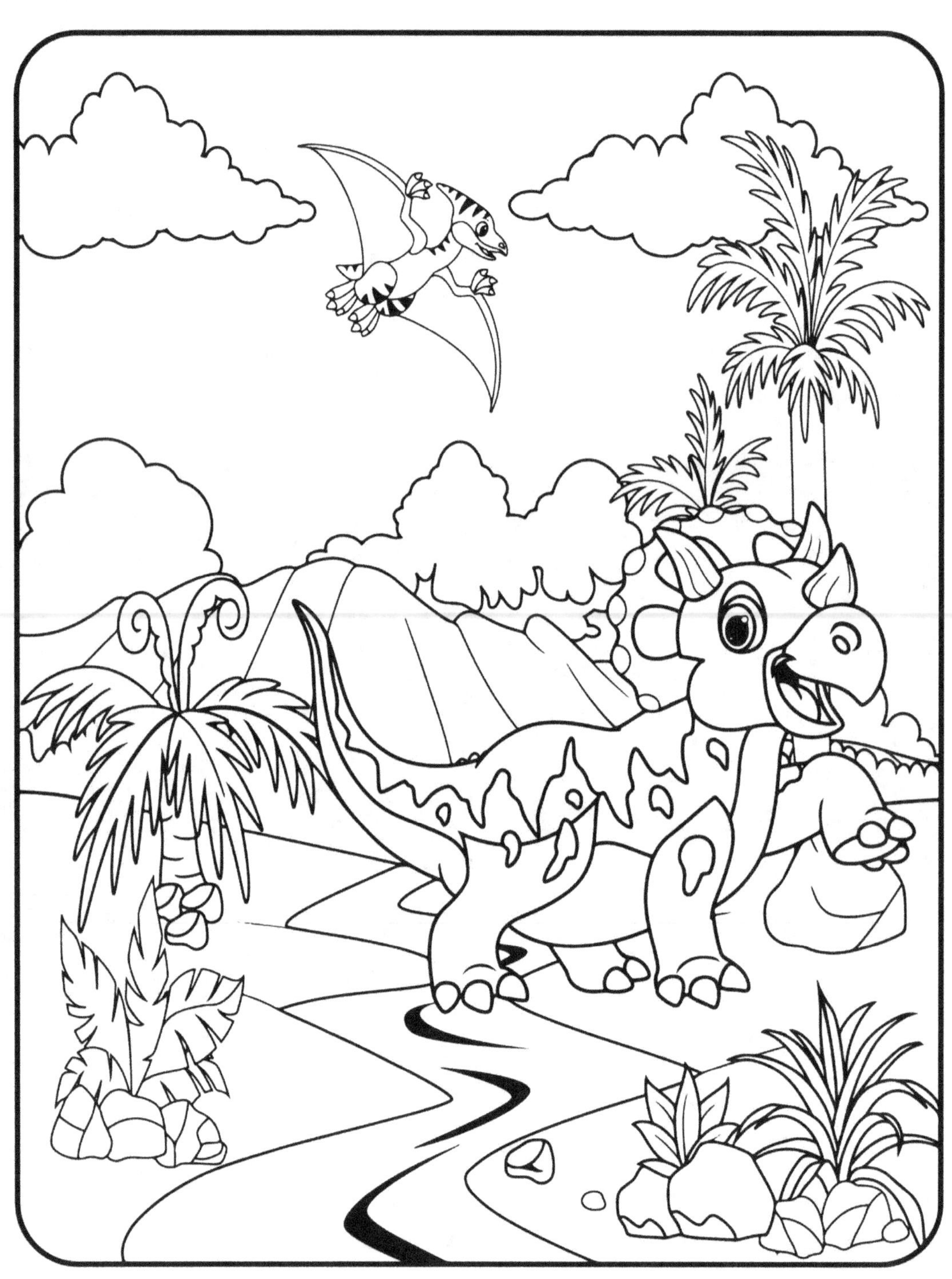

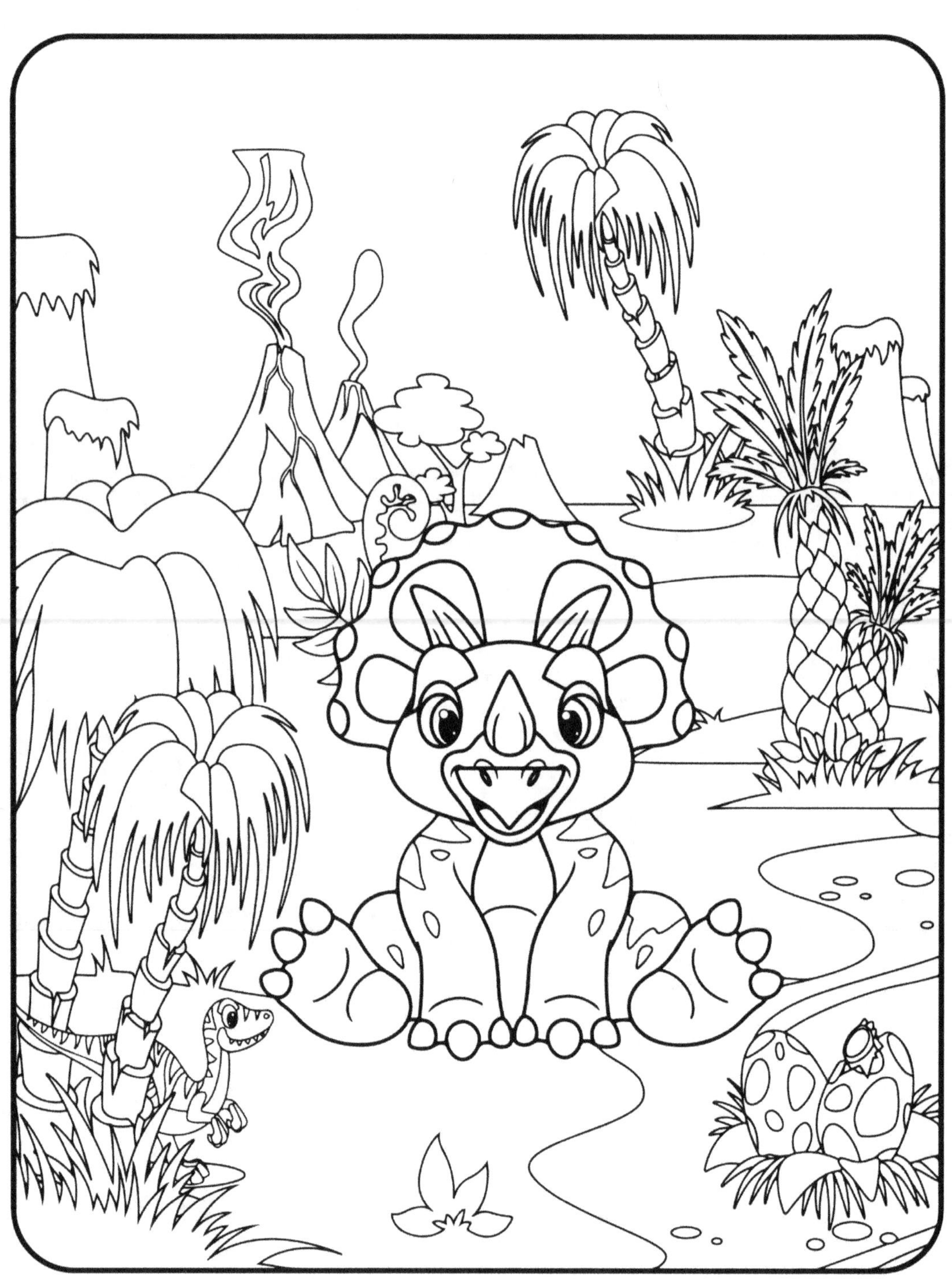

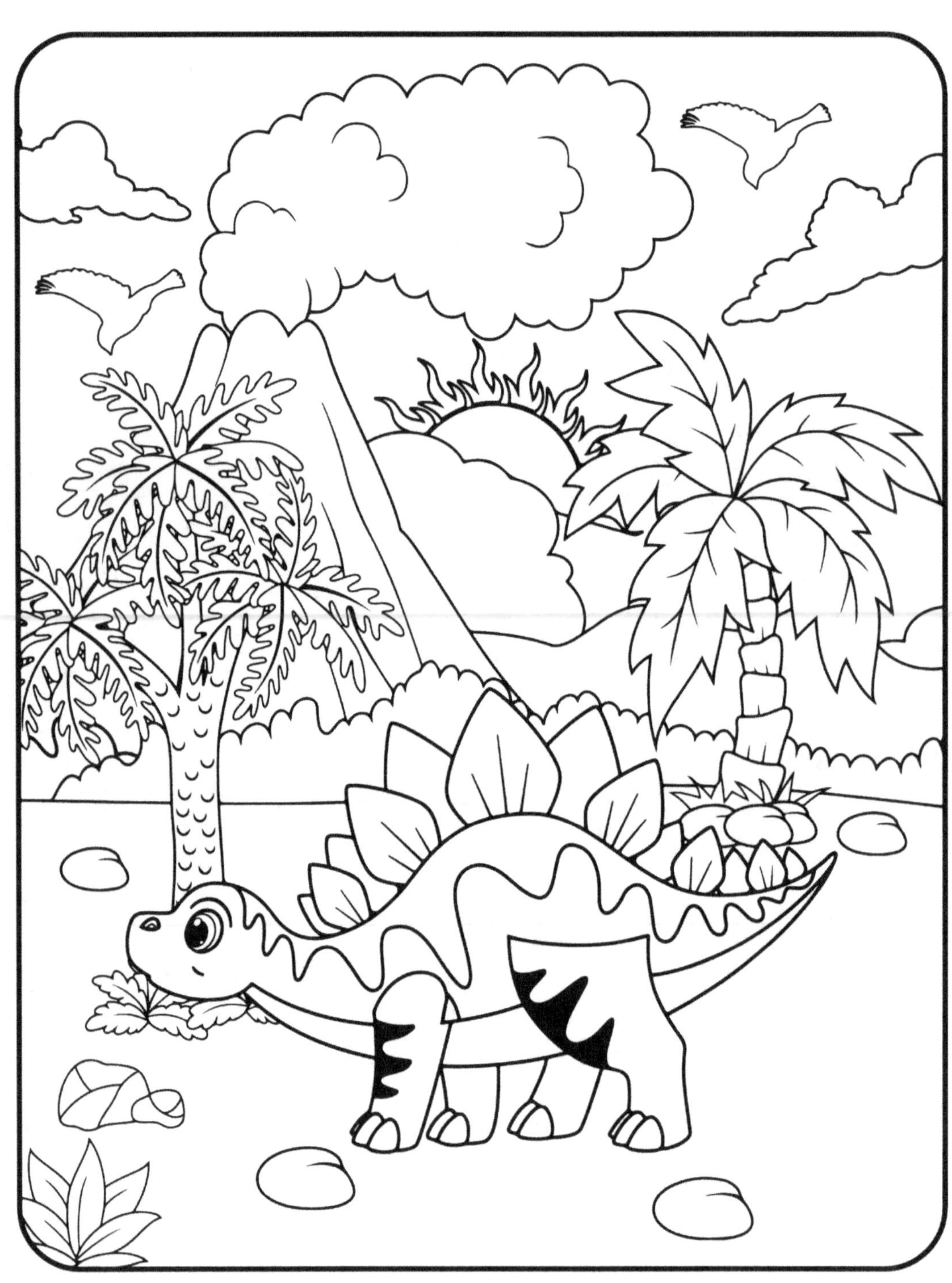

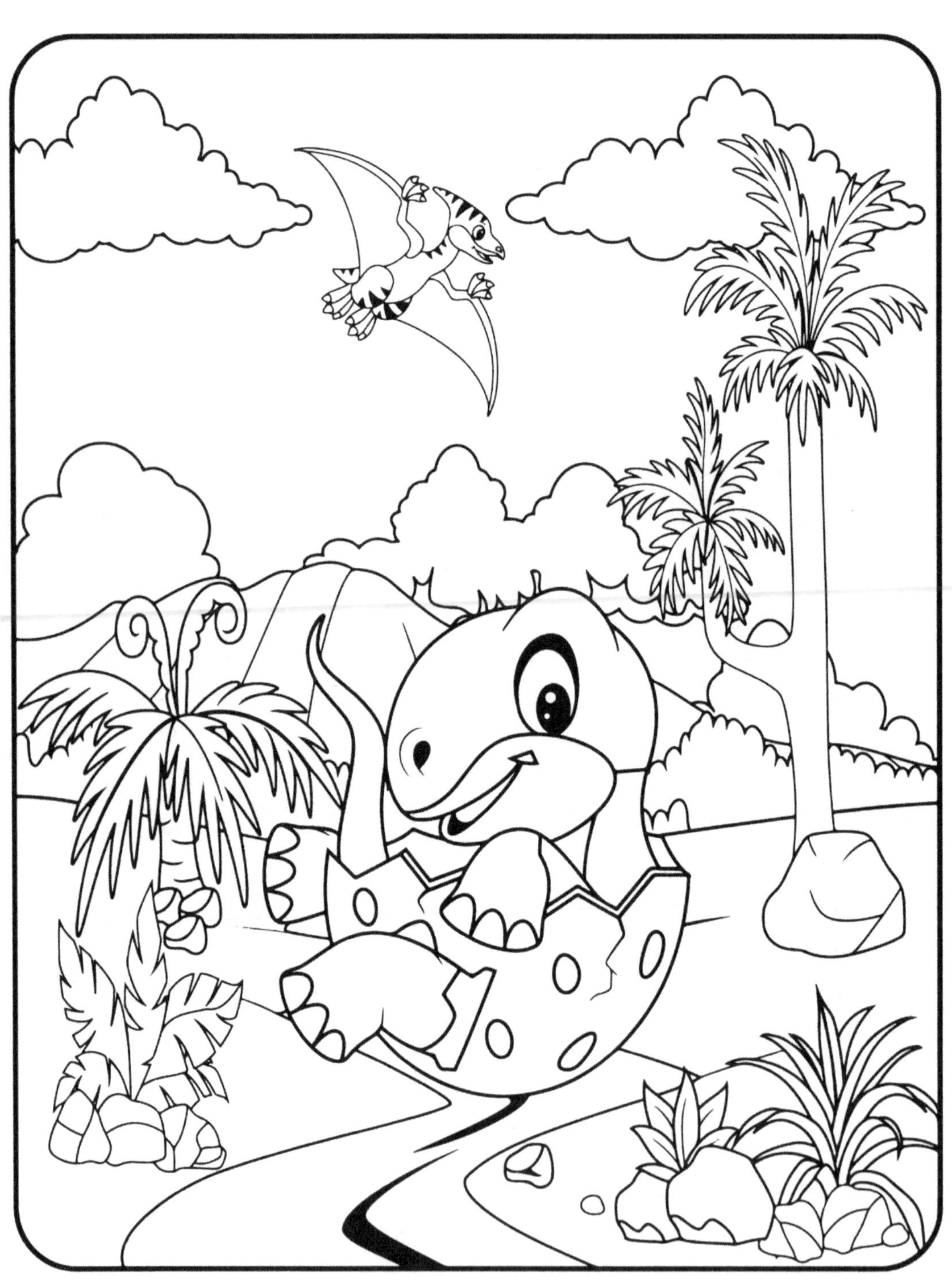

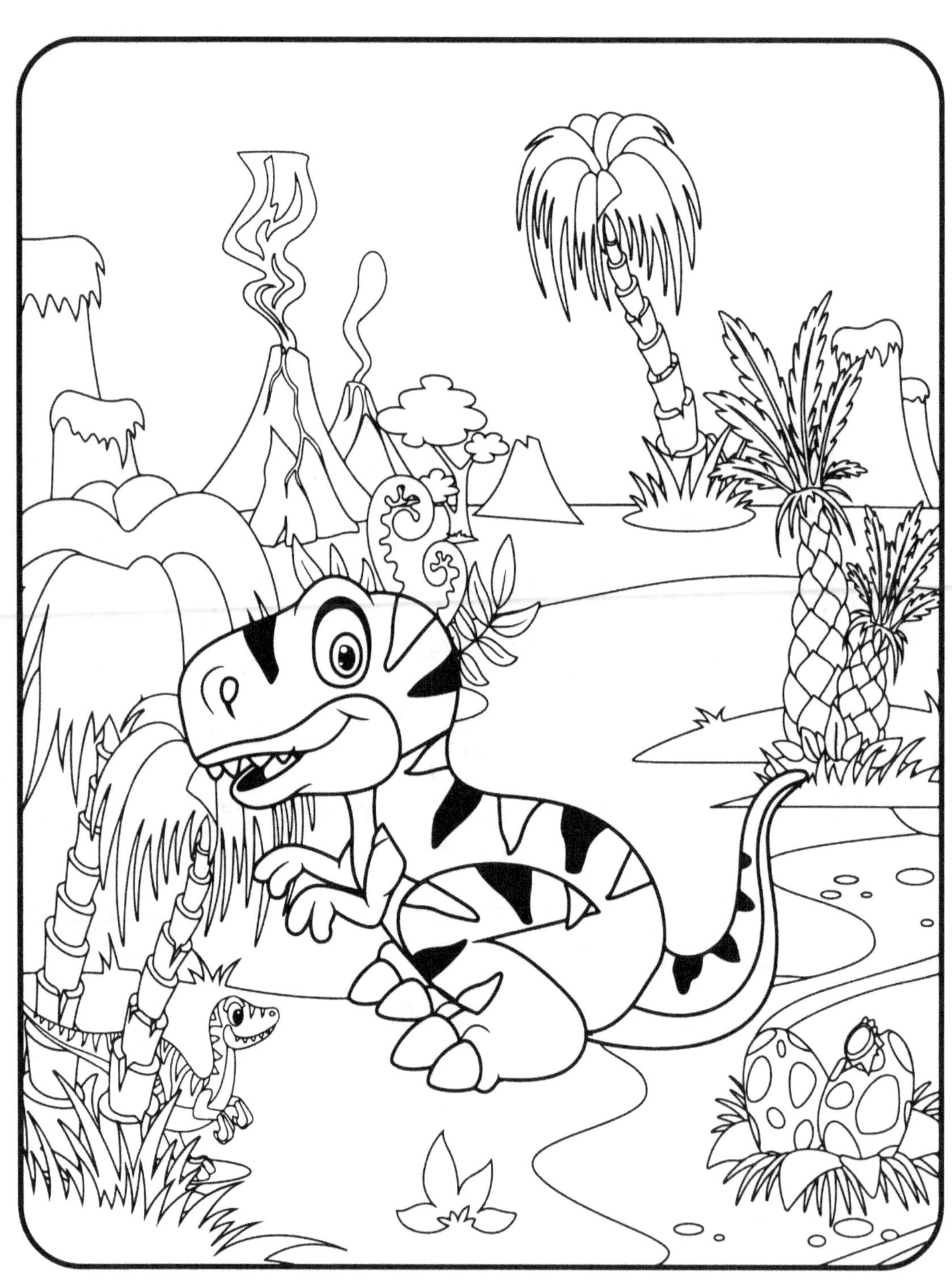

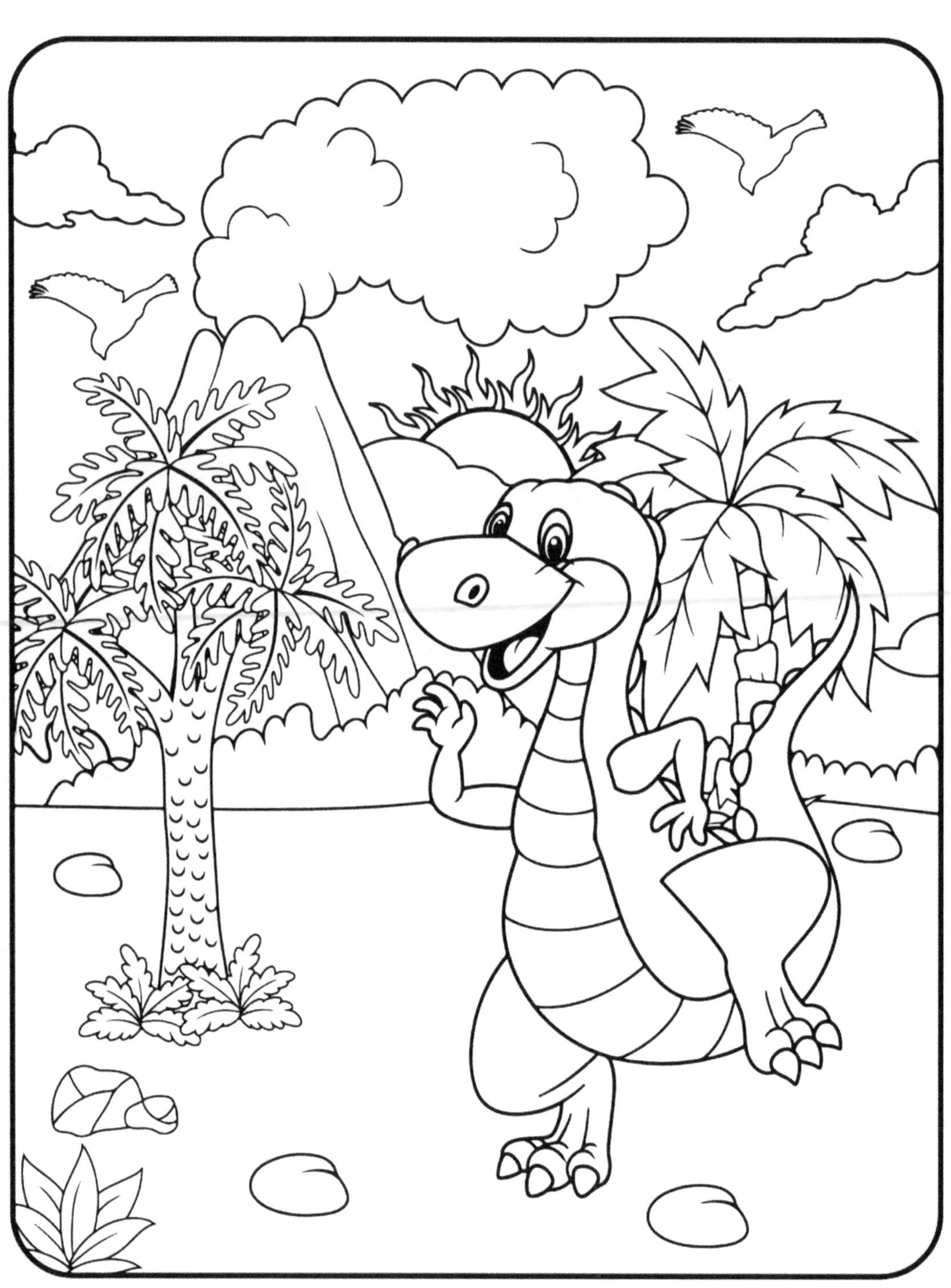

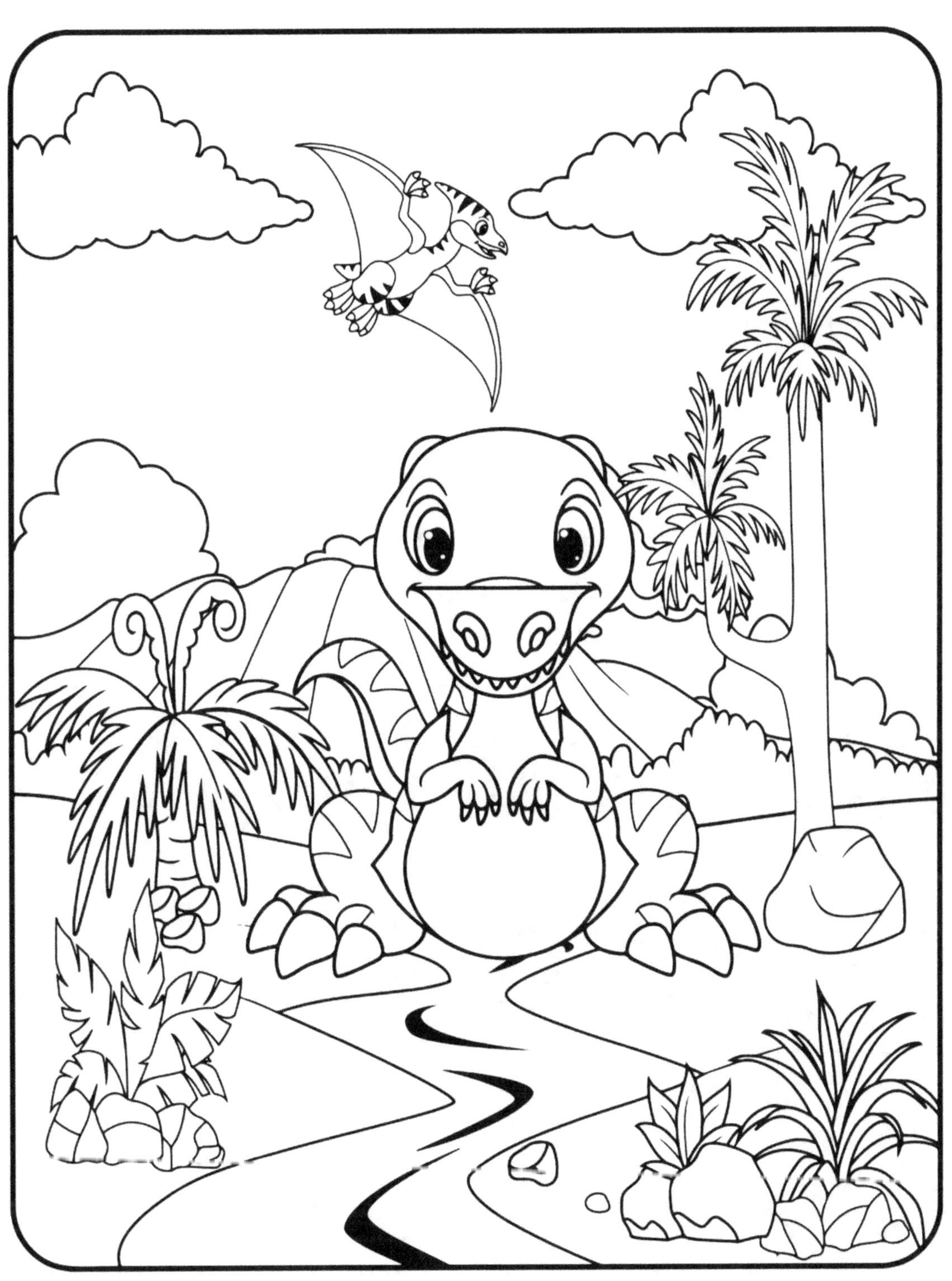

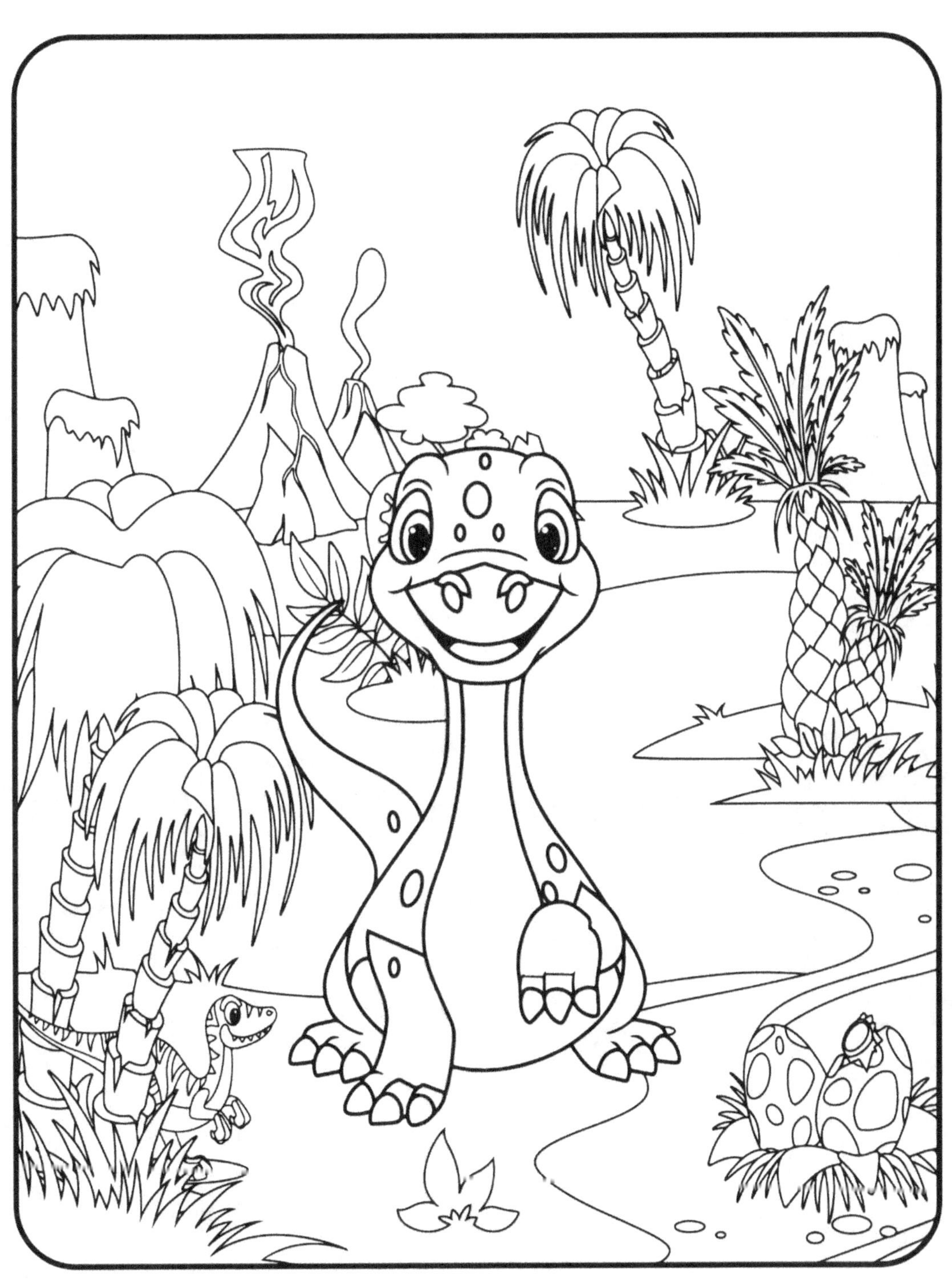

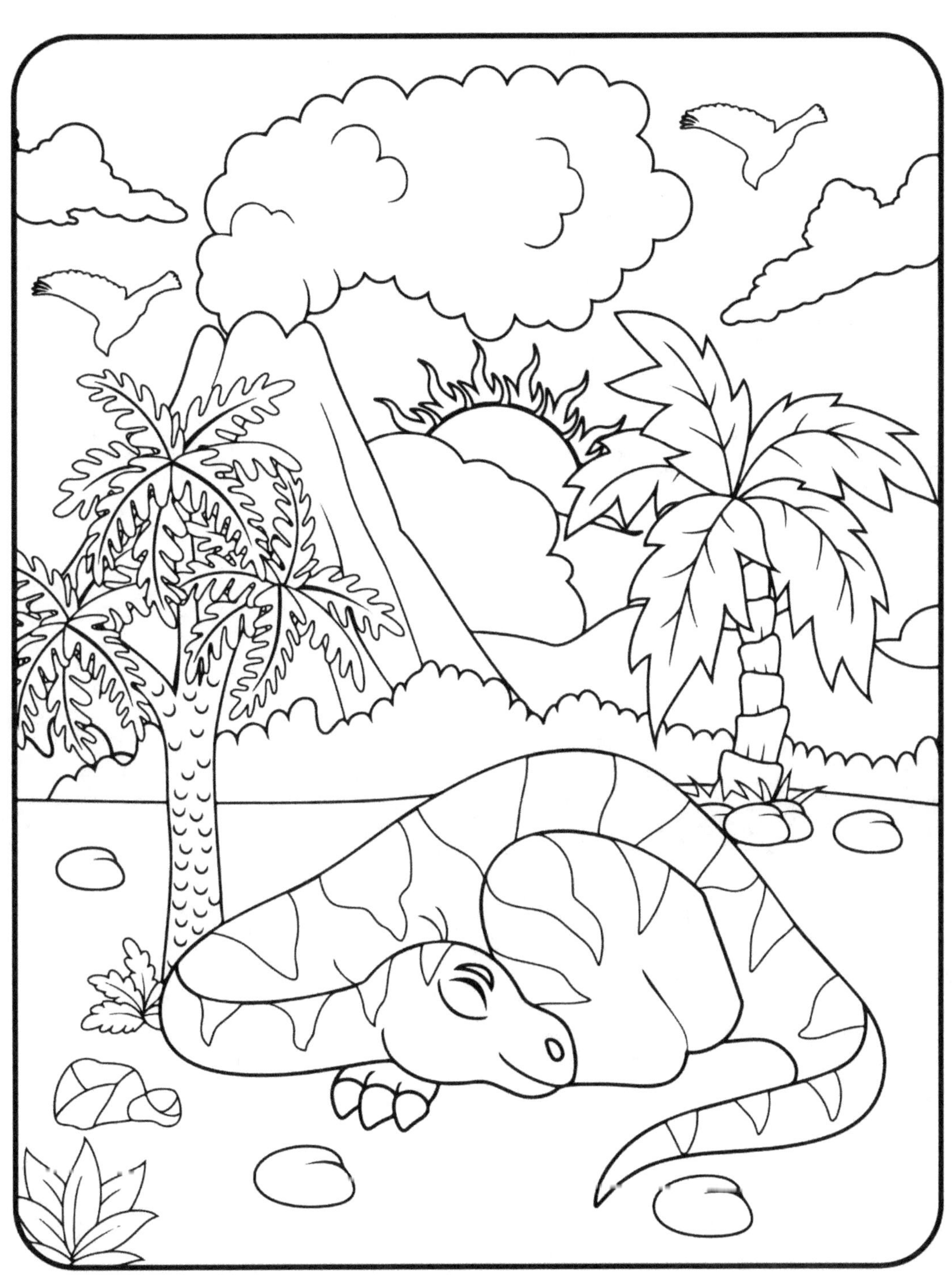

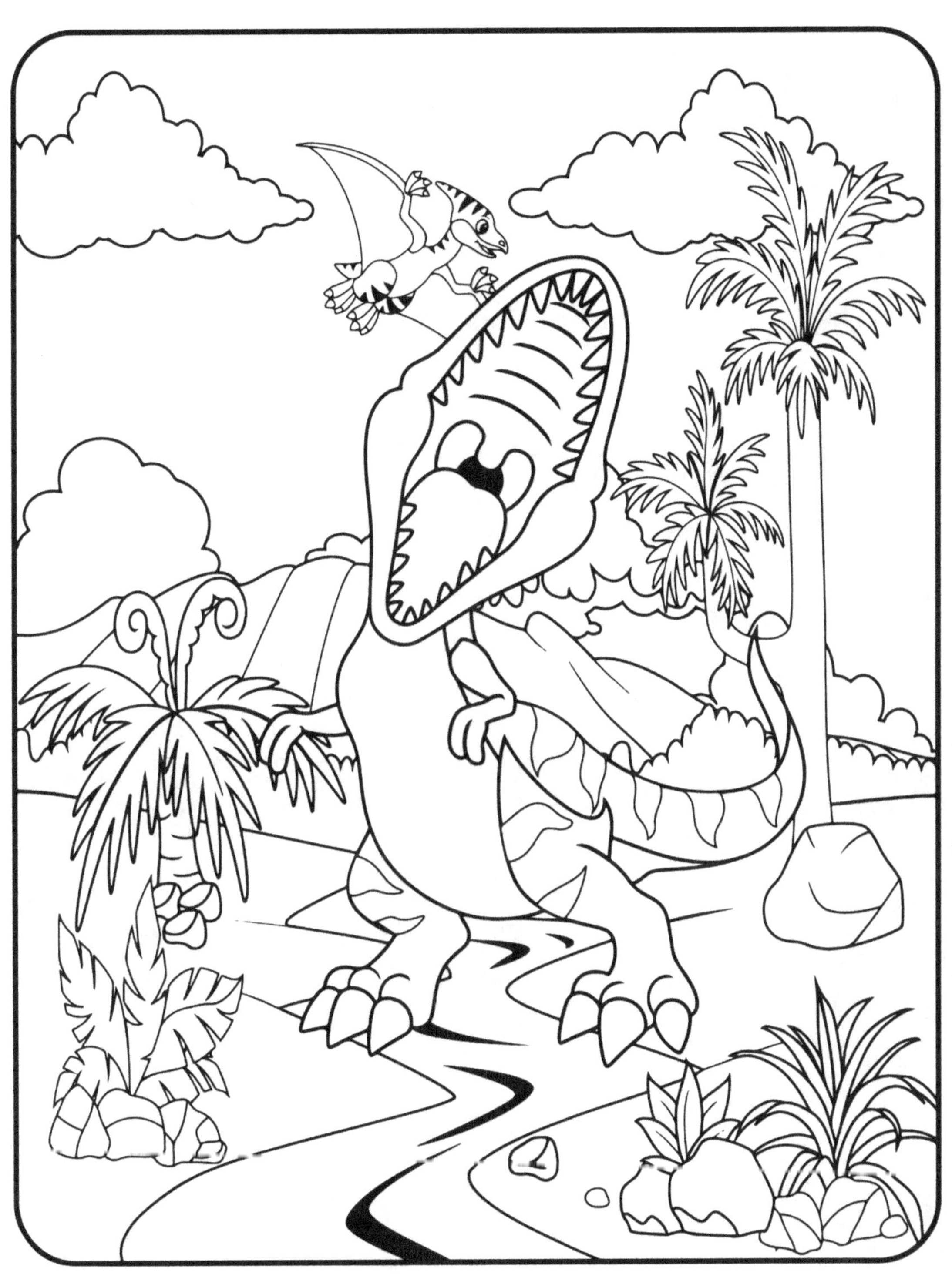

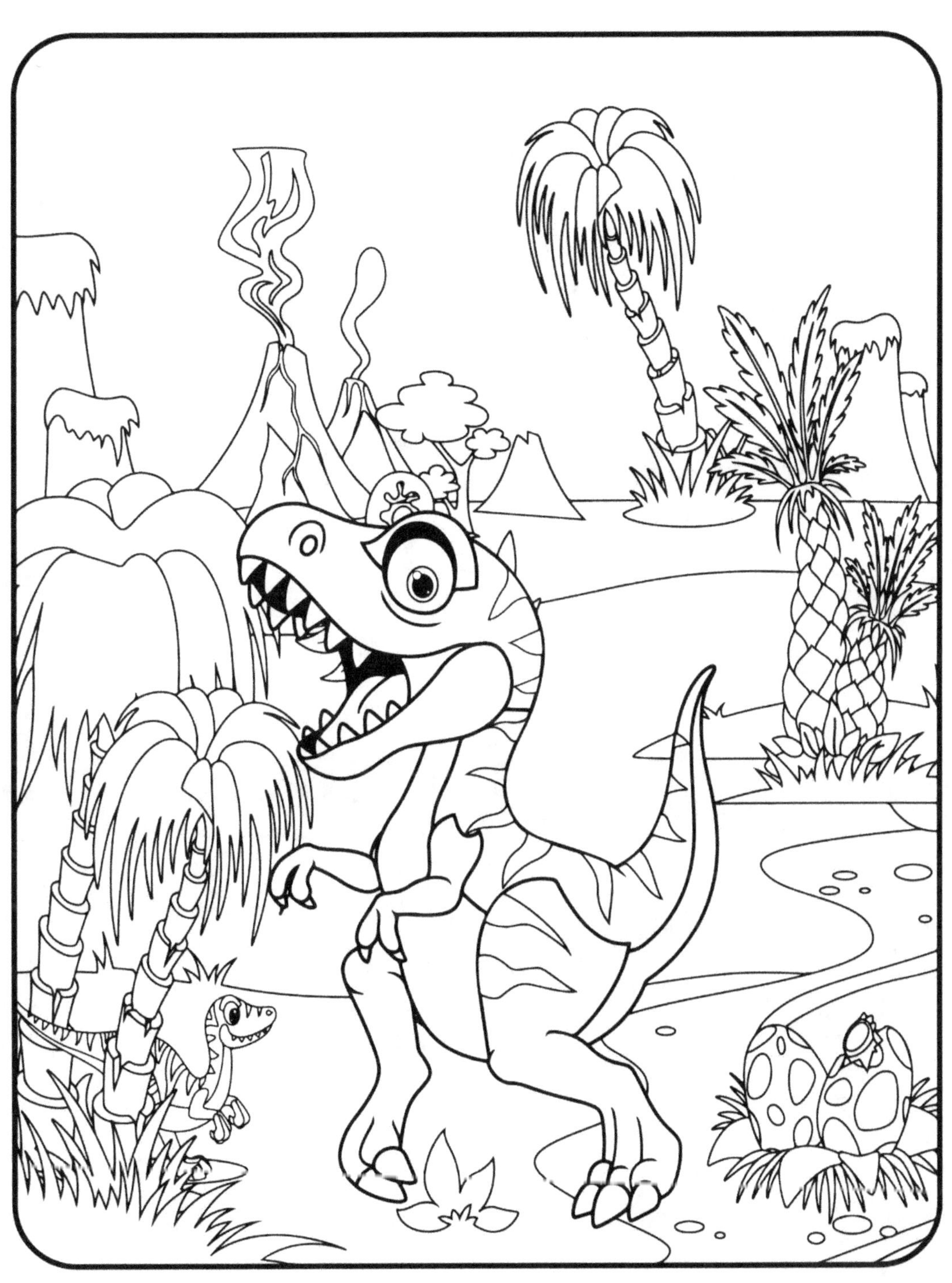

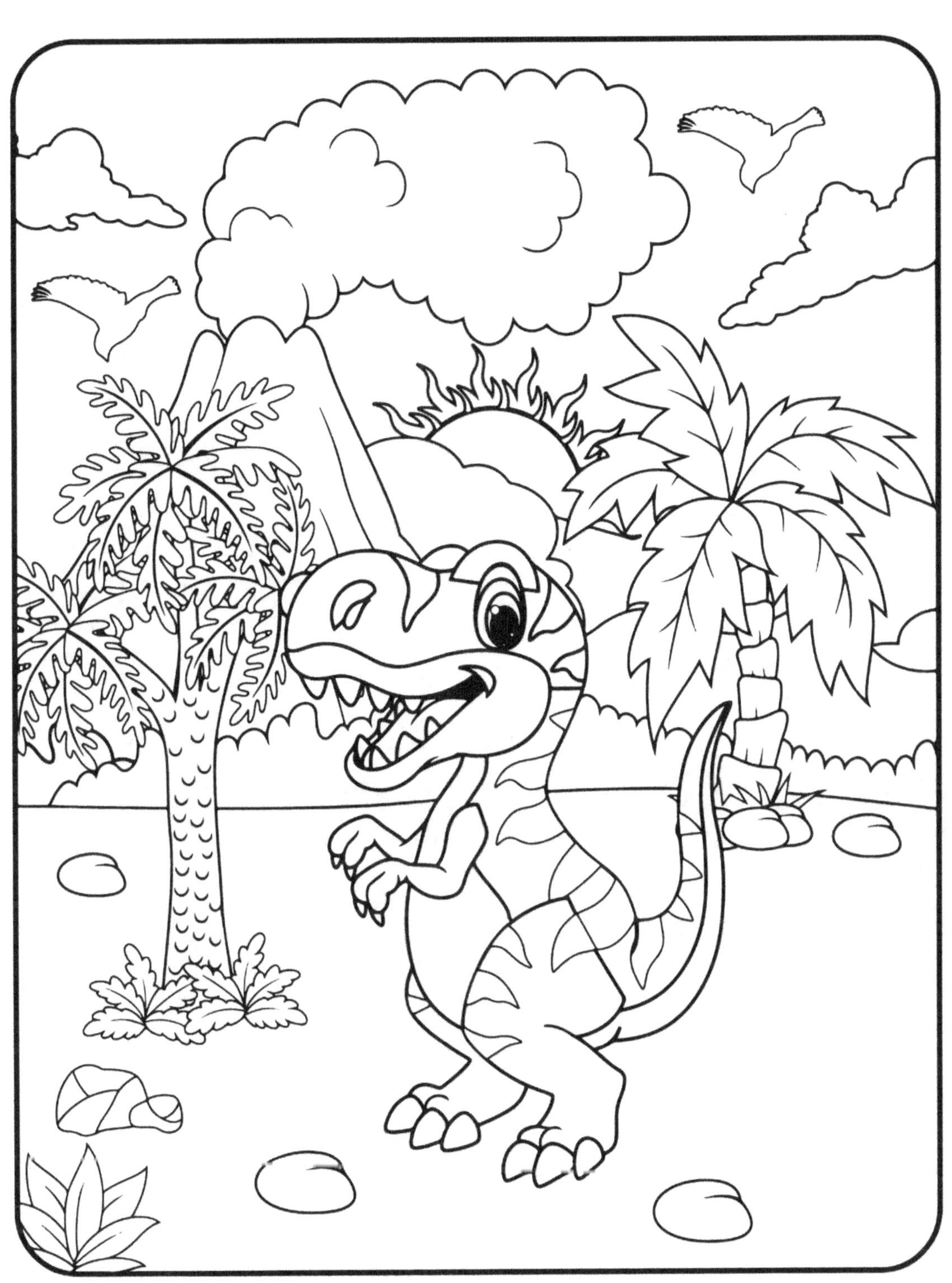

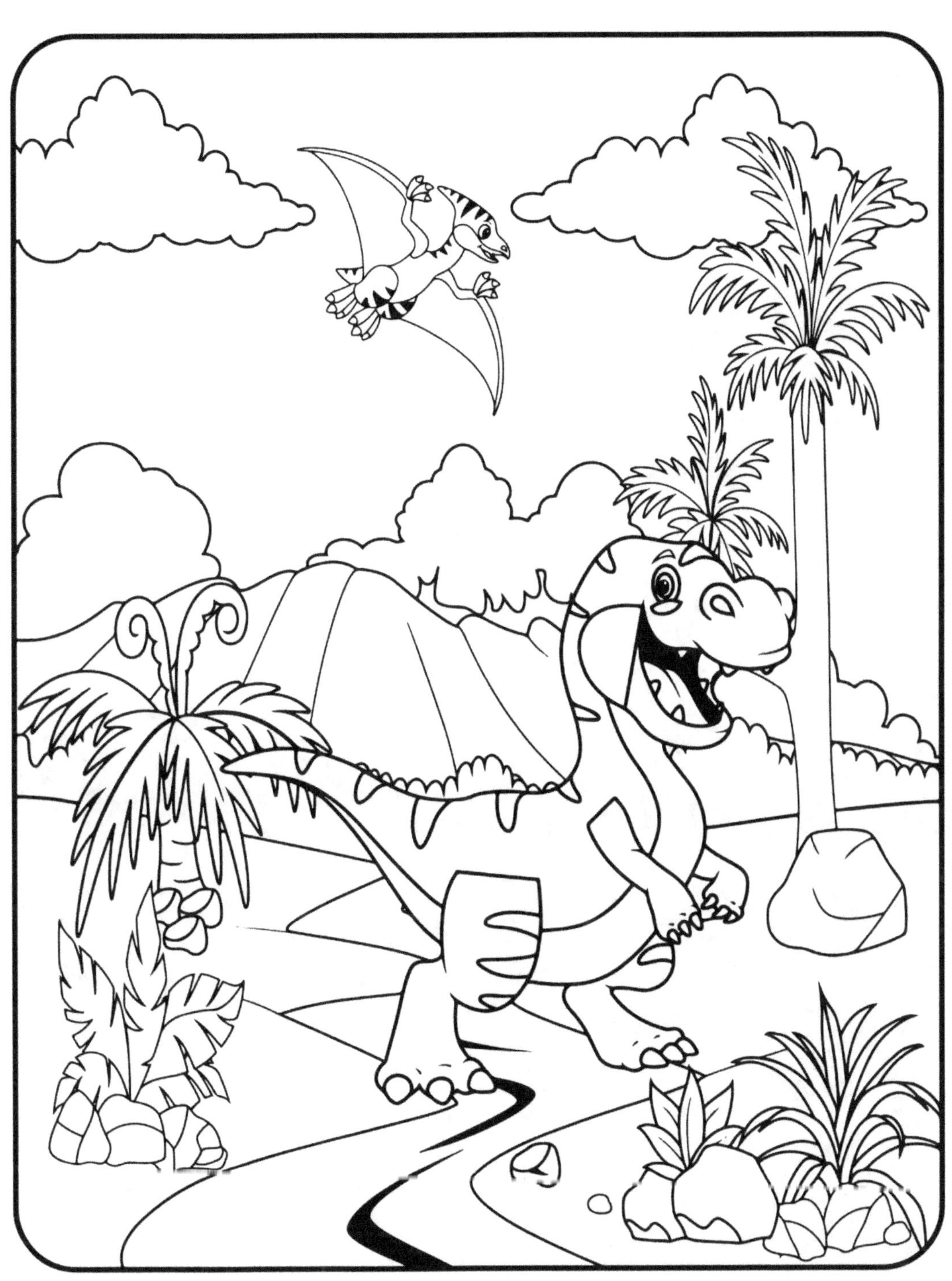

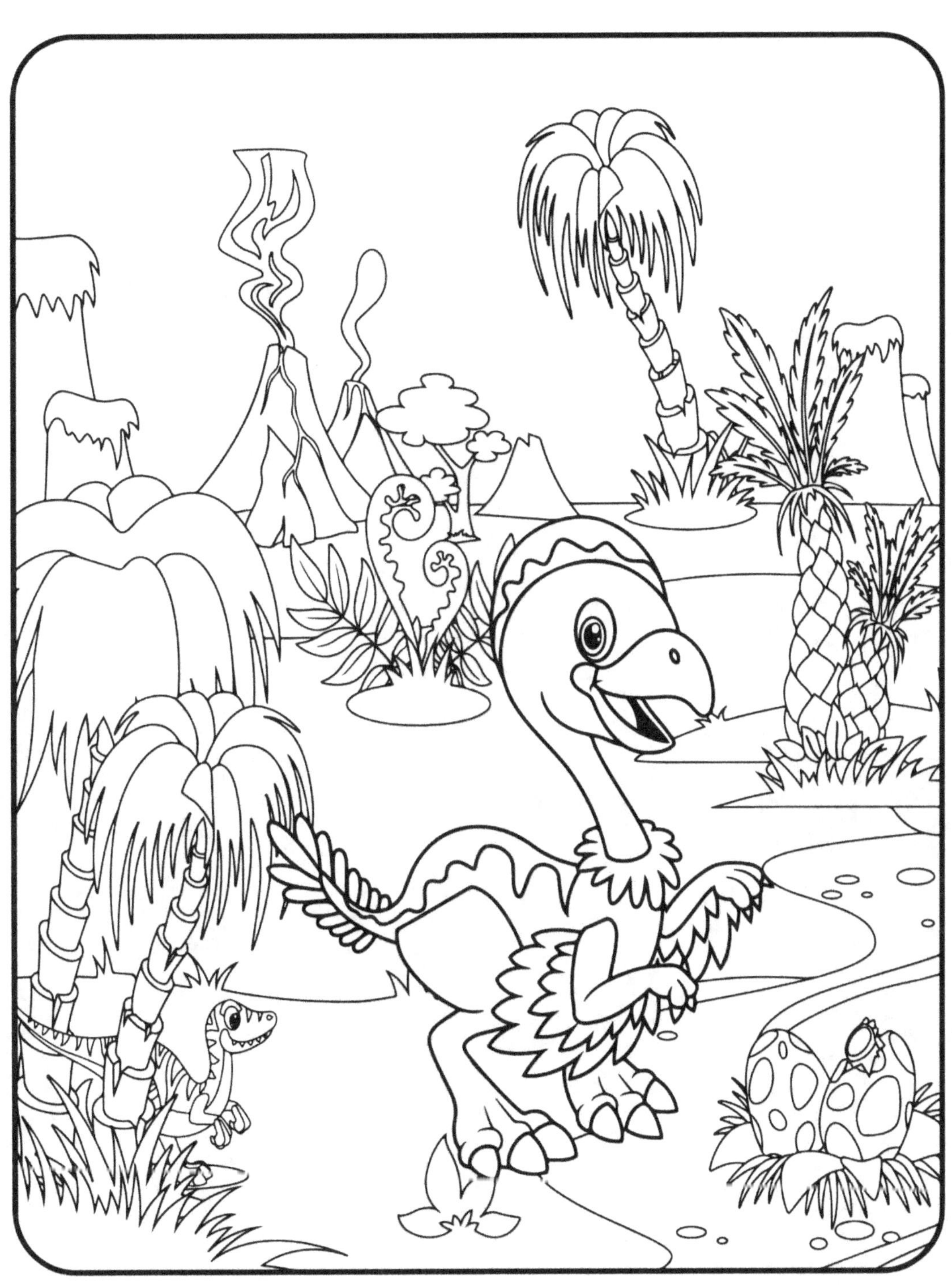

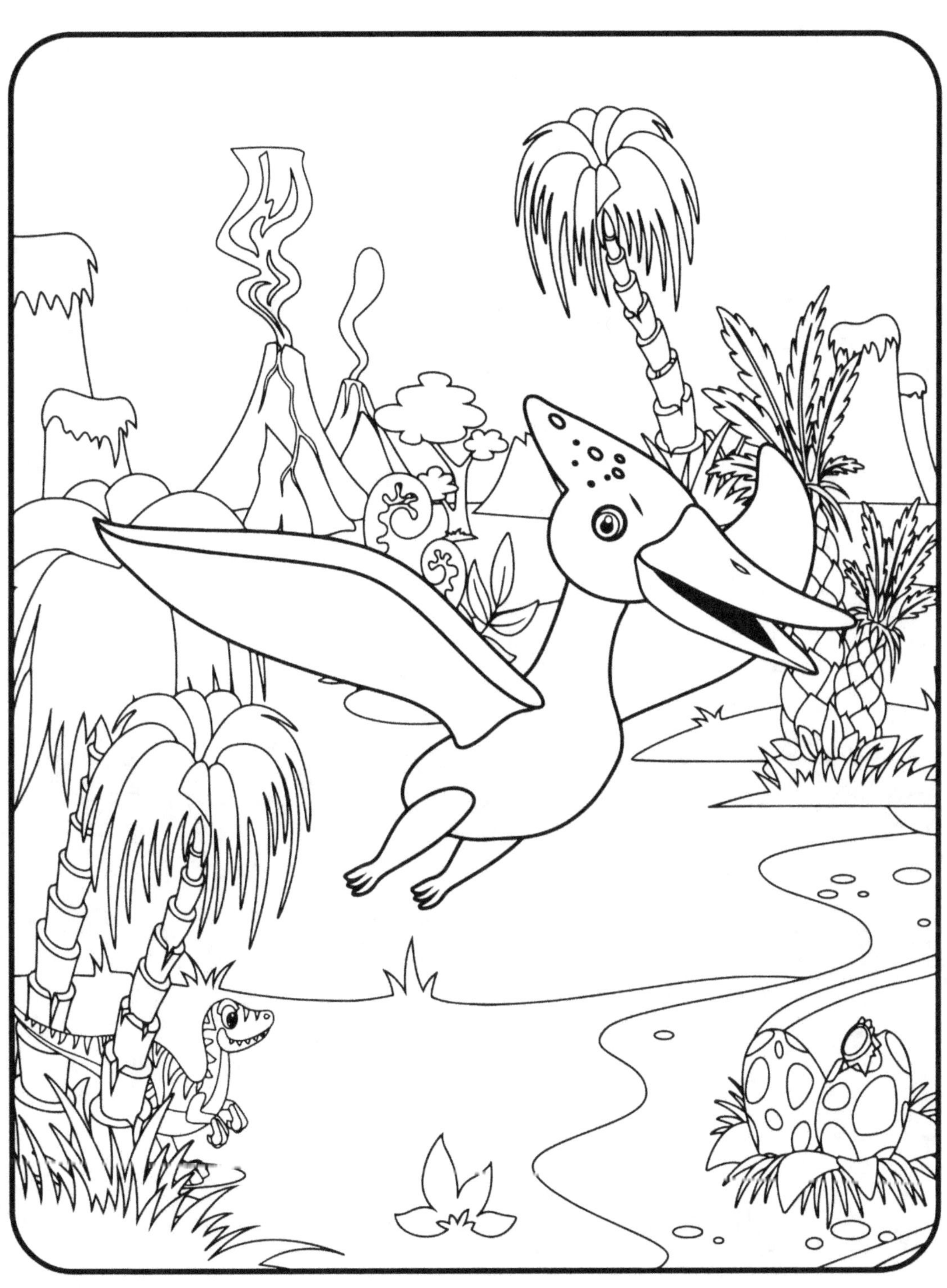

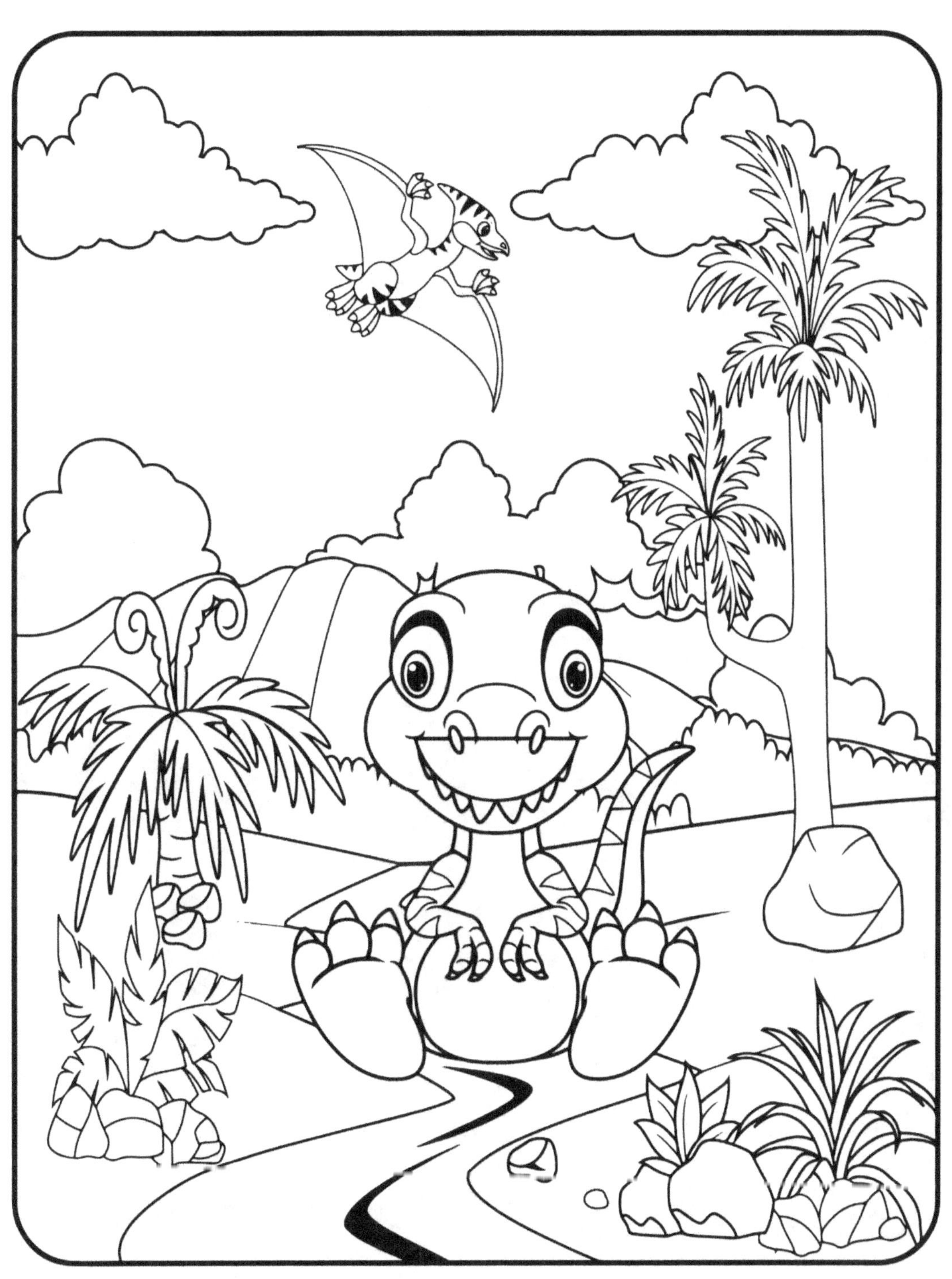

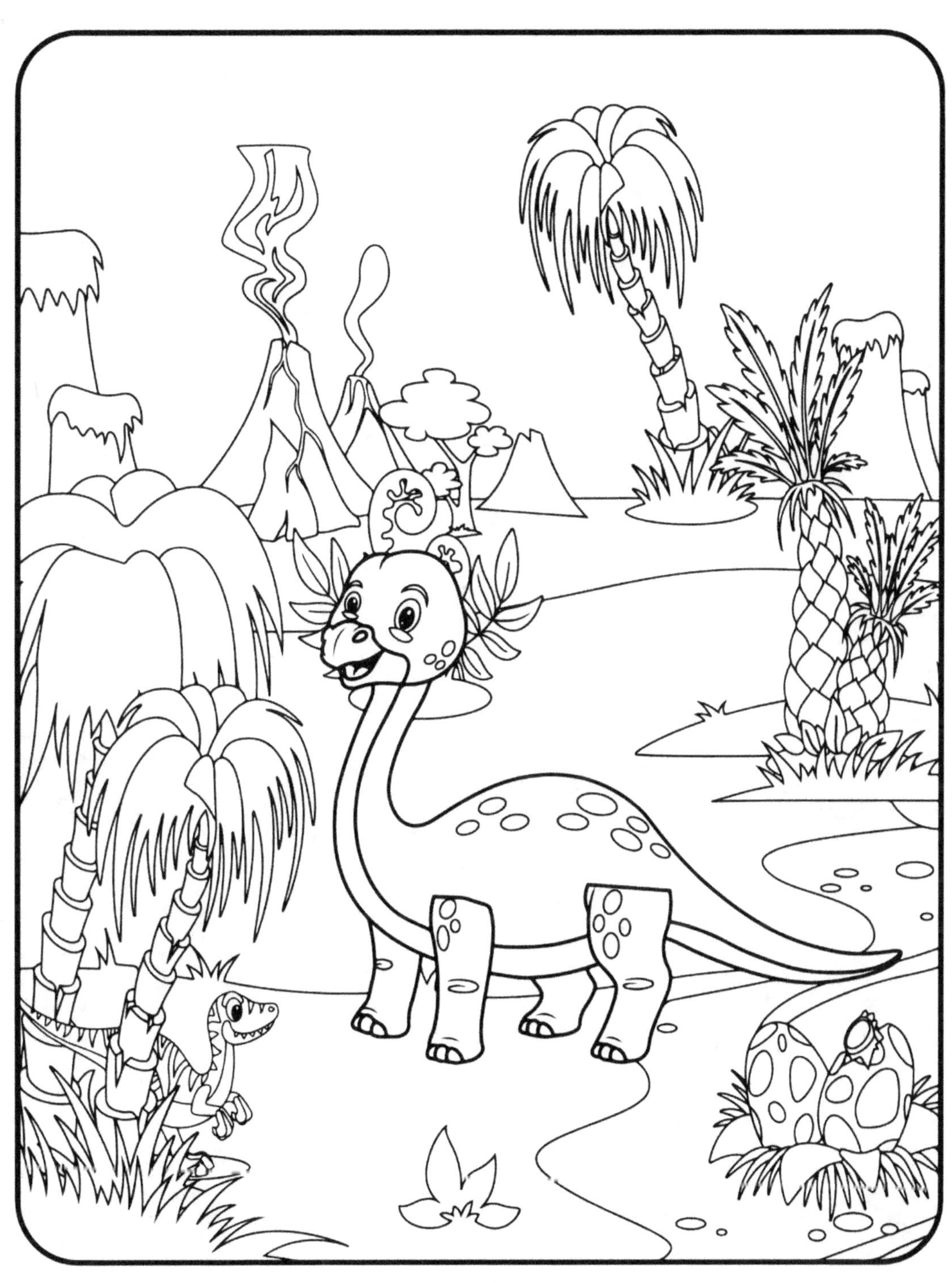

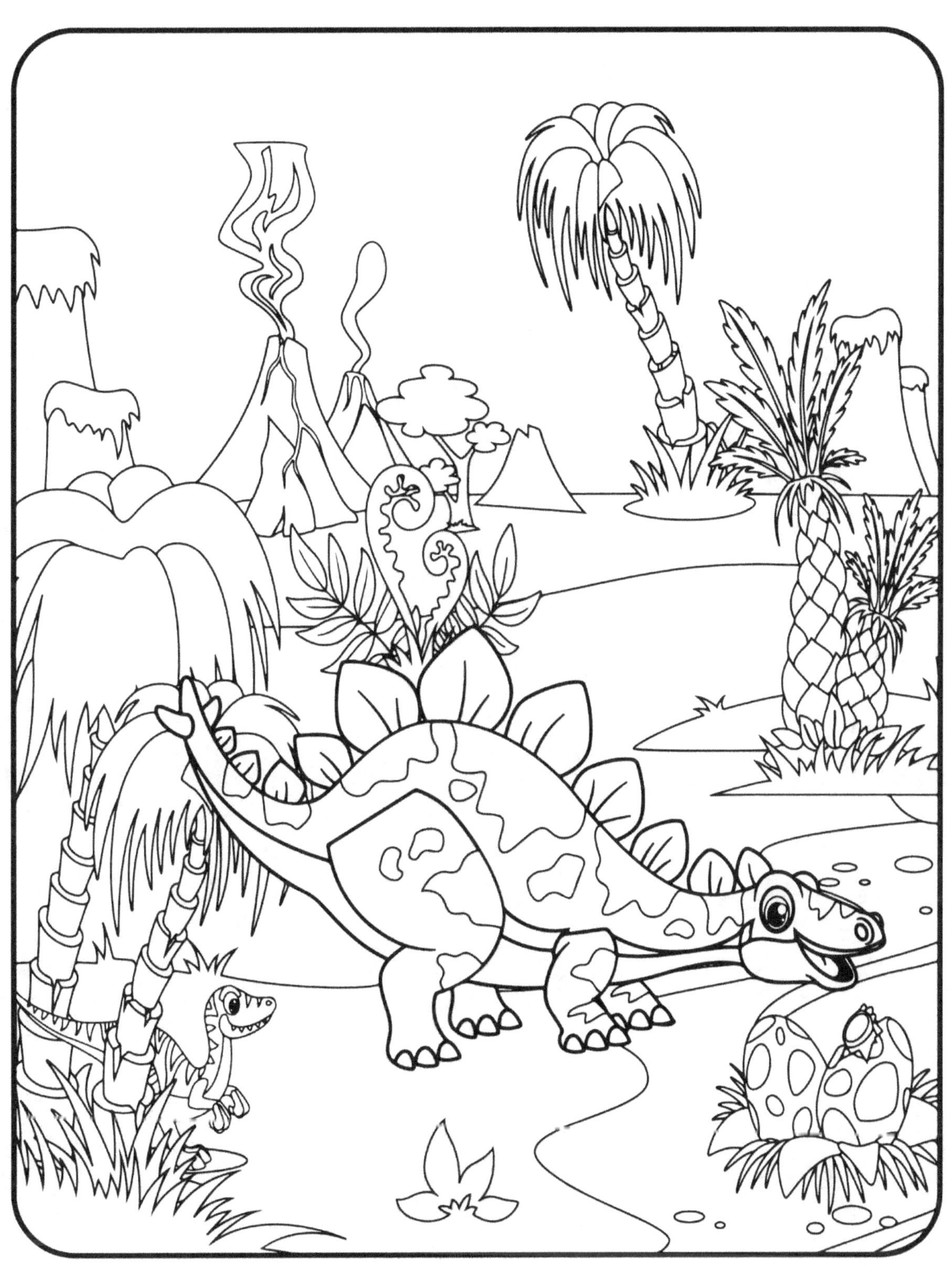

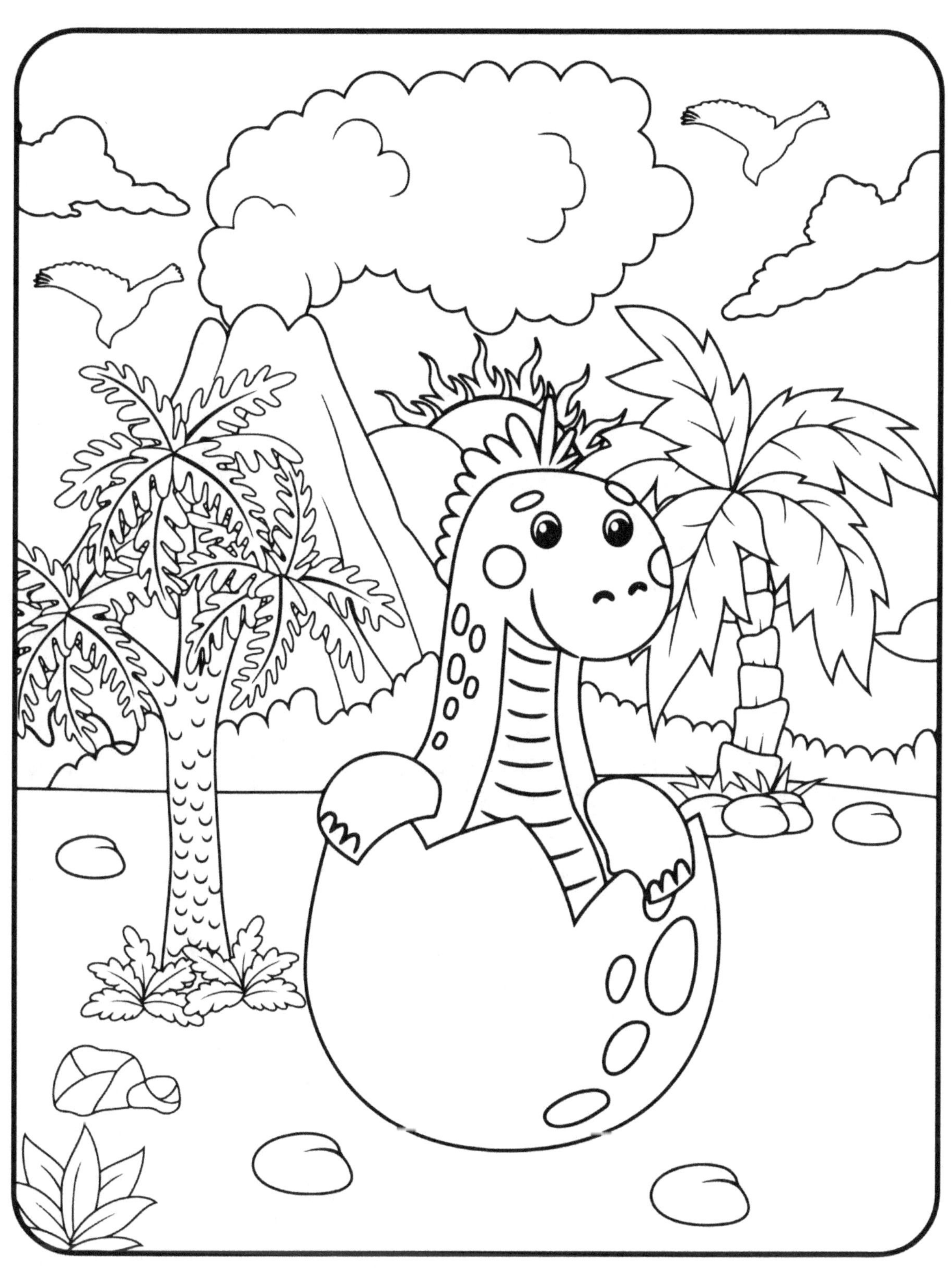

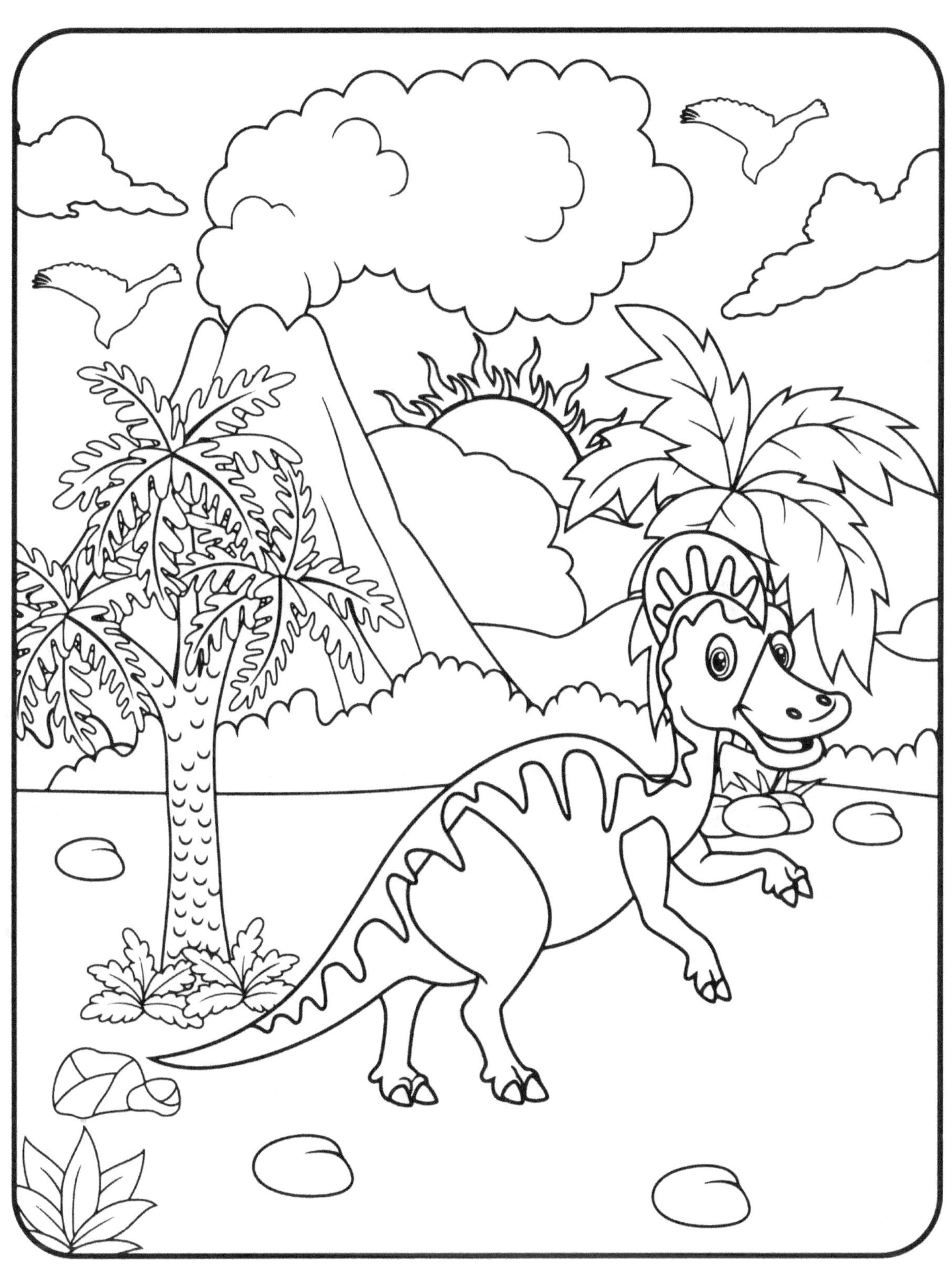